FREE MEN OF AMERICA

FREE MEN
OF AMERICA

By EZEQUIEL PADILLA

An Alliance Book

ZIFF-DAVIS PUBLISHING COMPANY

CHICAGO • NEW YORK

It is exceedingly fortunate that the Americas are united in their resolve to defend, against all aggressions, our continental doctrine of equality, of law, of mutual respect and decorum. This doctrine of peaceful and just relations constitutes the only hope for the salvation of the civilized rules of joint international life, so necessary in this martyred and bleeding world. Nothing separates us in this America of ours. The differences that may exist among our countries are superseded and blended in with the mutual and lofty aspiration permanently to establish a continental life of assured friendship and reciprocal respect in which reason shall predominate over brute force and peaceful co-operation over mechanized destruction.

MANUEL AVILA CAMACHO

T *Preface*

HE STATESMAN, WHEN HE WRITES ABOUT CONTEM-
porary events and personages, faces a dilemma all too obvious.
He is rarely able to disclose his special knowledge to the public.
His duties as a public servant immediately conflict with those
as an author. In one case, words and deeds must conform to the
requirements of public policy. In the other, the obligation is
to discover and state as much of the truth as possible. Usually,
even in the case of memoirs, books by leaders of state are so
full of reticences and caution as to be superficial, and likely
as not banal.

These criticisms do not apply to Dr. Padilla's book, which
is the refreshing exception to the rule. Quite the contrary, here
the dual functions of authorship and statesmanship, far from
injuring each other, are successfully utilized to the benefit
of both.

Except when he describes so vividly his air-trip to a Pan-
American conference, Dr. Padilla is so intent on his theme
that the reader is scarcely aware that the words are from the
pen of the Mexican Secretary of Foreign Affairs. At the same
time, the account is enriched by the special official opportunities he enjoys. By this work, Dr. Padilla not only gives greater
dignity and worth to high estate, but he has produced a real
author's manuscript, frank, outspoken, readable and exciting.
Free Men of America is a courageous book, based on wide
experience, deep knowledge and scholarship and written with
the fire of conviction.

Thus, Dr. Padilla stands in the tradition of the great
Domingo Sarmiento of Argentina, that remarkable statesman
of the past century, who democratized and renovated his country, and whose numerous works, though he was head of the
state, are illuminated by candor, honesty and noble purpose.
I believe Thomas Jefferson, were he alive today, would be glad
to sign his name to this book of Padilla's.

For it is a book that concerns itself, first and last, with human
liberty in all its aspects. He believes that liberty is the special
vocation of the Americas. Liberty has not always existed in

the Western Hemisphere, and for enormous sectors of the Americas even today economic liberty is still largely lacking. But out of previous struggles to abolish slavery, then serfdom, to end political and financial imperialism, armed interventions and dollar diplomacy and to create a free inter-Americanism, the love of liberty—the author believes—has become inbred in the American spirit and must and will triumph.

A book of this tone could hardly have been written by an Old World statesman, freighted with the tragedy and weariness of past and present, for here is the authentic note of the Americas: idealism, faith, ready optimism, forthright speech, a belief in the boundless opportunities of the future. This is not naiveté. Dr. Padilla has a thorough grasp of past and present realities, the problems, the difficulties, the various possibilities.

Precisely here—for me—Dr. Padilla's work has its greatest value. He does not shirk from his task, but definitely, even remorselessly, and always with tact, he points out the previous mistakes in both United States and Latin American policies. If he may offend a few stiff-necked sensibilities, no true patriot here or in his sister republics will have any other sentiment than gratitude. The author is not interested in the slightest in stirring to life any past controversies or in harboring any ancient resentment; history for him is valuable only as a guide for what is to be done next; and if he shakes a few skeletons, it is merely that he may indicate how great is the progress already made toward inter-continental harmony and to lay down a program both idealistic and practical for the Western Hemisphere. This is tied in capably with a broad philosophical approach and a plan for world international relations.

Mexico has long taken the leadership in seeking the solution for many of the problems that apply to the whole hemisphere, and Dr. Padilla is a worthy spokesman of those policies and a worthy spokesman for Latin America as a whole. He knows the needs of his own land and of the other countries of the Americas. Certainly this book is far superior—in its elevated tone and in its practical approach to actual problems of the Latin American world and of the United States in relation to that world—to anything I know of in recent years from an

"American" pen, official or otherwise.

Dr. Padilla deserves to be heard for, upon the proper solution of the problems he presents, may well depend the future safety and happiness of the United States both in world affairs and in matters pertaining to this continent. He deserves to be heard so that we may never again commit the blunders of the past. He deserves to be heard because he tells of the true obligations of both Latin America and the United States in the creation of a bonafide inter-Americanism. He deserves to be heard so that for a while we Americans may think, not so much of what we ourselves need and want, but in terms of the whole continent. He deserves to be heard because he knows that the Americas cannot be free, that a sound inter-Americanism cannot be created, while a large part of the population is deprived of proper health and educational standards and proper economic security. He deserves to be heard because he knows that the Americas cannot be free so long as whole countries continue to be merely semi-colonial appendages producing raw materials under disadvantageous conditions.

Some may not agree with all of Dr. Padilla's ideas and proposals, but no one can disagree with his facts or the actuality of the problems he sets forth. Here is a bold amplification of the Four Freedoms: the extension of them squarely into the economic sphere, the steps necessary eventually to put them into operation throughout the Western Hemisphere.

And unless the liberties and justice which Padilla proclaims are established on our own side of the water, then the war will have been fought in vain and the next one will be close at hand.

CARLETON BEALS

Contents

W Introduction

HEN IN JANUARY, 1942, I LEFT THE CITY of Mexico to attend the Conference of Foreign Ministers of the American Republics at Rio de Janeiro, the tragic smoke columns of Pearl Harbor still hung heavy against the clouds of war. Although more distant than events in Europe, the grim self-sacrifice of the garrison at Wake Island and the heroic resistance of Manila's defenders brought home to every American heart deep awareness of disaster.

An American nation had been brutally set upon. One of the twenty-one flags of the continent of brotherhood had been treacherously assailed. In the battles that followed, men born on our hemisphere were defending their honor, their integrity and the principles common to all the free peoples of the earth.

The speeches of Prime Minister Churchill and President Roosevelt on this occasion were like a dialogue—the basic terms of which had been set forth in the Atlantic Charter—on the disasters that had taken place, and at the same time an affirmation of a noble vision and unshakable faith in ultimate victory.

At Miami a mammoth clipper, with a long record of flights, was waiting for some of the Ministers or their representatives, to carry them down to Rio de Janeiro. A few minutes before climbing into the plane, I met Ambassador Fernández Concheso of Cuba; the Minister of Foreign Affairs of Ecuador, Mr. Tobar Donoso; the eloquent Ambassador of Colombia, Dr. Gabriel Turbay; the Minister of El Salvador, Mr. Héctor David Castro; and the Foreign Minister of Honduras, Mr. Julián R. Cáceres. I had already met Mr. Sumner Welles, Under-Secretary of State, as we had exchanged calls the previous day.

I glanced over the brief data in my notebook on the chairmen of the delegations to the Third Meeting of Consultation of Ministers of Foreign Affairs of the American Republics. I was much impressed by the terse sketch of Sumner Welles' personality: "Under-Secretary of State. Harvard graduate. Entered diplomatic service during Wilson Administration. First-class mind. Well-grounded in diplomacy; a negotiator of great skill.

Specialist on Latin-America. One of the real creators of the Good-Neighbor Policy. Distinguished bearing, blue eyes, cold expression."

Those of us who later saw Sumner Welles in action at Rio de Janeiro were greatly surprised to find beneath the seeming chill of his manner a man of a keen, ardent feeling, unusually responsive to the nobler emotions.

When the clipper took off, after the morning mists had dispersed, we all crowded to the portholes to gaze at the landscape below.

Beneath us the beauties of Miami spread out. Once-barren reefs, flooded and dangerous marshes, had been turned into a flourishing, delightful city. In the distance, palms and pines swayed in the breeze. It brought to mind the verse of Heinrich Heine; it was a symbol of the unity of nations.

When the magic of the view had faded and before we sighted the Bahamas, we began to get acquainted with one another. Some of the group were personages high in the political world, of whom I had heard on frequent occasions, among them expert economists whose youth and early renown impressed me.

In our narrow confines, where for three days we were to share a common destiny, the newspaper men soon attracted my attention. They were writers of international reputation, eminent leaders of public opinion in the United States. Many had participated in the great events of contemporary history. Some had described the fierce battles of the present war, as eyewitnesses under a hail of lead and steel, like the English painter, Turner, who lashed himself to the mast, the better to paint the fury of the storm.

My talks with these correspondents were both pleasant and instructive. Journalists are gifted with imagination. We must not expect chemically pure truth from them, but we cannot hope for this from life itself. With them I commented upon the wonders of the view spread out before us ten thousand feet below.

We alighted on the water off Puerto Rico. Before we came down, the curtains were drawn over the clipper's portholes. The secrets of the defense of the fortifications there had to be screened from any prying eyes.

We were allowed only ten minutes to see the city. As we were climbing back into the airplane to resume our journey, I said to Carl Spaeth, "Perhaps some time, in the audacious modern manner, we can write a book packed with facts for others to consult, entitled *My Ten Minutes in Puerto Rico*."

It was night when we dropped down to Trinidad. The next day, from a height of ten thousand feet, we caught a glimpse of the Salut Islands. Among them lies Devil's Island, off the coast of French Guiana, where Captain Alfred Dreyfus was confined.

Soon we saw in the distance the sweltering colony of misery and death that for centuries has served France as a prison for criminals convicted of serious offenses. On its sea-battered cliffs might be written the fateful words of Dante's Inferno: *"Lasciate ogni speranza, voi ch'entrate"* ("Abandon hope, all ye who enter here").

Is it not an anachronism, I thought, that penal colonies should still exist in these free lands of the Americas? More than a century and a half ago Benjamin Franklin asked the English what they would think if the United States were to send rattlesnakes to their Islands. Why should our territory be an abode of slavery and suffering?

When I first sighted the coasts of the South American mainland, thoughts of Simón Bolívar came into my mind. He lived in a day when the dream of reconquering the Americas was one of the pet ambitions of the Holy Alliance.

Once again history repeats itself. Not this time, however, in Metternich's salons, buzzing with the intrigues of the diplomacy of those days, "in a world apart, amidst lights and loves supernal, far removed from human misery and high above the region of the storm." Now it is Berchtesgaden, that forbidding lonely recess, whence orders to lay waste, to bomb, to destroy ruthlessly, pour forth incessantly. Among the plans drafted there is that of the subjugation of the Americas.

Despite the similarity between the circumstances of that day and this, what deep differences have been created by the passing years! Not so much in the actual dreams of conquest that obsess the leaders, as in the means they command to convert their violent ambitions into deadly realities.

In Bolívar's day, distance was an impregnable defense against even the boldest plan of invasion. The world was then an archipelago of silence where all news arrived late. The effect on the imagination of a naval battle in the Antipodes was as of something legendary, outside the realm of time, like the battles of Salamis or Lepanto.

Today, everything takes place in the full view of all the world. Man is actually a spectator who witnesses, as they take place, the events of history, however far away they may be. He is at the same time, willy-nilly, a soldier on the firing-line. There is nothing now to protect him, neither mountains nor oceans.

Submarines sailing the seven seas and airplanes roving the broad skies make us realize more and more each day that the safety of isolation belongs to the past. It has faded away like the successive panoramas our airplane left behind it.

Suddenly we found ourselves flying over the jungle of the Amazon. Those few hours of the trip gave me a sense of the grandeur of the Universe such as I had never experienced before. The delta of the Amazon, sprawling over two hundred and forty-odd miles, is an astounding piece of cosmic handiwork. Here we see Nature at her fiery labors. Boundless rivers, unending forests, all under the torrid rays of a blazing sun, resemble a colossal laboratory whence the clouds emanate, like cosmic nebulae spiraling ever upward.

Afternoon was falling when, after ten hours of steady flight, we came to the mouth of the Amazon, to that seething cauldron over which the God of Genesis seems to preside. Suddenly we beheld an unforgettable spectacle. A stream of thick cirrus clouds, dazzling white, moved across the forest from one edge of the horizon to the other, like a broad river of snow, through the perfect, amazing channel the winds opened for it.

The setting sun turned the twilight into a flood of fire. It was like the glow of a forge, a blast furnace, pouring over the vast plains. And below, the mouths of the Amazon seethed and roared incessantly. From time to time, the sun's fiery disc pierced through the clouds, as if some sacred rite of the Universe were taking place, something for which the human tongue could find no words, a magnificent symbol of the America that is coming into being.

As we flew over those immense uninhabited forests, past mighty rivers and valleys, thoughts of landing airplanes and parachutists came to mind. It would not be difficult for them to land and establish bases with the help of organized fifth columnists.

The same idea beset us whenever we gazed down at the far-flung coasts of the Americas. For thousands upon thousands of miles around the edge of the American Continent there are any number of sites suitable for submarine nests or the landing of troops.

In their remoteness, their silence and innocent complicity, the coasts, the valleys, the mountains of this vast America might well become points of vantage for enemies boring from within in combination with invaders from without. One need only remember that there are in Brazil 300,000 Japanese, and that 800,000 Axis subjects could be organized there, to realize the danger inherent in the configuration of our continent if a New World divided against itself should open the way to potential invasion.

First, a groundwork of propaganda, then subversive action in the different countries, the fostering of friction, the neglect of all plans for the common defense, would create a Heaven-sent opportunity for the enemies of democracy to destroy our cities, spread discord among our people and hinder and block any effective action in our bewildered, confused continent.

The present submarine campaign in the Atlantic, which, despite continental watchfulness and solidarity, has sent hundreds of thousands of tons of shipping to the bottom, gives us a faint idea of what totalitarian aggression might be, could it count on the complicity of American peoples divided among themselves.

If a federation of American nations was a noble ideal in Bolívar's times, it is a pressing and imperative duty today. The watchword of every free conscience must be to combat, as if it were the plague, anything and everything that might lead to the fratricide, destruction and enslavement of this continent.

I was sure, as we alighted in Rio de Janeiro, that similar thoughts must have been in the minds of the assembled Ministers of Foreign Affairs, disturbing the delightful impression produced by the beauty of that genial, radiant metropolis.

Foreign Secretary Oswaldo Aranha was waiting for us on the dock. He was the kindly host on that great occasion. A true Brazilian, of noble bearing, a distinguished man of the world, his courtesy, his ability and his intelligence were to weave the bonds of cordiality.

Rio de Janeiro is one of the most beautiful cities on the face of the earth. If, as has been said, Egypt is the gift of the Nile, the Brazilian capital can be called the gift of the sea. Nowhere else has the ocean so busied itself tracing upon the beaches such wonderful filigree work, such capricious designs, such intricate smiling curves. The sea washes the very foot of the mountains. Its endless lapping has carved out tiny islands, miniature peninsulas, toy bays. And here, as everywhere else, the jungle lurks in the background, waiting to seize upon the land again.

As one gazes down from the plane, the overpowering impression of the Amazonian exuberance gives way to admiration and delight at the matchless charm of the spectacle that is Rio de Janeiro.

Nearly all the great cities of Brazil are close to the Atlantic Ocean. Her people always look out upon the sea, turning their backs to the mountains, unlike so many American countries, particularly Mexico, which, contrary to her own interests, keeps her eyes fixed on the hills, never deigning to turn toward the sea.

Can this be the reason why the Brazilians, blessed with a land so magnificent and so privileged, are kindly, peaceful, tolerant and conciliatory?

Were the Spartans indifferent to death because their harsh, sombre land offered them little? And are Brazilians essentially peace-loving because they already have all they could ask for in their land flowing with milk and honey?

Brazil is as mighty as the Amazon and as smiling as Rio de Janeiro. She is the land of cordial men.

Was not this the best of all auguries for a conference that was to be decisive on the destinies of the Americas?

This book is to some extent the outcome of that memorable experience. It has been written with the haste with which messages pass between ships fighting the same battle on the high seas. It is not dedicated to the experts, or the learned, or the philosophers. It aims at only one thing: to bring home to the masses of the American nations a feeling of responsibility and an exultant and creative determination to undertake the noble task of building up the indissoluble unity of the Americas.

T

Slavery · I

O GRASP FULLY THE FACT THAT WE REALLY ARE laying the basis for the brotherhood of this continent, we must understand that our peoples are emerging only now from the darkness of a past in which international relations rested upon force, exploitation and distrust.

We are gradually rising out of a world that was organized for aggression and warfare. The invasions, unjust wars and shameful exploitation the peoples have suffered are the substance of which history has been made. Moreover, those abuses are recorded all too often as glorious events.

The philosophy and consciousness of national groups were not forged for peaceful enterprise. The straitened economy in which the nations lived led them to attack the wealth of others in order to create their own prosperity.

It is necessary, therefore, to look upon these iniquities of the past as a consequence of the political and economic systems by which the world has been governed, rather than as deliberate decisions by the nations themselves.

The Americas have blazed their trail to freedom through the dank forest of servitude. Their determined and progressing fight to achieve the dignity of man has at times resembled the prolonged struggles of ancient Rome to gain her liberties.

Among the continents subdued by imperialist Europe, surprisingly enough neither Africa, nor Oceania, nor Asia, have ever succeeded in proclaiming their sovereignty. Yet the Americas, although more closely knit with the colonizing continent, have won their independence. The reason is that freedom is America's vocation. The vigor shown by this hemisphere in combating every threat of domination springs directly from its traditional struggles against the various forms of servitude it has experienced.

To appreciate that our own security can be founded only on the confidence we repose in a new civilization, it is necessary to recapitulate briefly the chronicle of the fight against slavery in the Americas. Only in this way is a review of the past helpful: to compare it with the present and lay out a course for the future.

When the Spaniards came to Mexico, they found there the beginnings of institutional slavery. Nearly all prisoners captured in war were destined for human sacrifice on the altars of the temples. In Peru slavery was unknown. Nor did it exist among the aboriginal population of Brazil or in North America.

Father Bartolomé de las Casas in Mexico, and a Jesuit father, Manuel de Nóbrega, in Brazil, induced the Kings of Spain and Portugal to decree all Indians freedmen. The generous voice of these friars succeeded in bringing about legal prohibition of native enslavement. In actual practice, however, the lot of the Indians was not improved, for they were reduced to a condition of serfdom.

By such devices as the Mexican *encomiendas,* or allotments, the conquerors, with strength on their side, constantly flouted the royal orders. It was no easy task, in the silence of the forests or in the depths of the mines, to subdue merciless greed for profit or the inhuman cruelty of the overseers and agents on the plantations, by an edict from the other side of the ocean.

Hence the appeal of the friars in defense of the American Indian was a voice in the wilderness, and in those colonies insufficiently provided with native manpower, it produced an abominable fruit—the African slave trade.

In 1511, Ferdinand V ordered a large consignment of negroes purchased on the African coast shipped to the Americas. The success of this venture, from a commercial point of view, established the slave trade as a recognized institution for nearly four centuries.

Spain's example soon was followed by England's colonies in North America. Under the protection of the Crown and of local governments, the importation of slaves developed into an indispensable source of labor for the development of the new communities in the south.

Protests were quickly raised against this shameful institution. Richard Henry Lee of Virginia, before the independence of the United States, lifted up his voice against slavery, in indignant tones that reveal his moral stature. His action was a worthy forerunner of the eloquent words of his fellow-citizens from that same State, George Mason and Thomas Jefferson.

On August 22, 1776, in the course of the debate on the articles of Confederation, Mason memorably declared, "By an inevitable chain of causes and effects, Providence punishes national sins by national calamities."

On February 12, of the same year, the Society for the Abolition of Slavery of Pennsylvania, of which Benjamin Franklin was president, had drawn up a memorial declaring that equality for all was one of the original rights of man. But before these ideas could triumph, several generations had to elapse and one of the bloodiest civil wars in the history of mankind had to be fought out.

Mexico was the first American nation to decree the abolition of slavery. This was done barely a month after Mexico's struggle for independence began. When Father Miguel Hidalgo y Costilla arrived at Valladolid in October, 1810, he ordered the Intendant, José María Anzorena, to issue a decree abolishing slavery and the payment of tribute by the Indians. December 6 of the same year, in the city of Guadalajara, he decreed the freedom of all slaves and fixed heavy penalties for violations. Finally, José María Morelos, in 1812, and President Vicente Guerrero, in 1829, completed the destruction of slavery in Mexico.

In Venezuela, also, the work of abolition was carried out very early. As of July 1, 1816, the Liberator, Bolívar, issued a decree summoning all slaves to military service, offering them their freedom, with compensation for their owners. One month later, in a document known as the Proclamation of Ocumaré, he decreed the freedom of all slaves.

In the Argentine, in February, 1813, and in Colombia in July, 1821, it was decreed that all children born in slavery were to be free.

In the United States and Brazil, slavery was an institution of much greater magnitude and importance than in the other countries mentioned.

Condemnation of slavery and the slave trade in the United States was passionately and forcefully expressed from the very outset of the nation's independent existence by the leaders of the fight for American liberty.

Washington in his will ordered that his own slaves were to be set free. Before that he had told Jefferson that "there is not a man living who wishes more sincerely than I do to see a plan adopted for the abolition of slavery." John Adams had declared his aversion to slavery and advocated adoption of all prudent means for its total and eventual extirpation in the United States. Similarly, Franklin, Madison, Hamilton, Patrick Henry, all disapproved of the slave system. Jefferson, at the first Continental Congress after the British forces had departed, proposed (March 1, 1784) to the Government of the area included within the northwestern states an ordinance providing that after 1800 there should be neither slavery nor serfdom. With reference to slavery, he said, "I tremble for my country when I reflect that God is just; that his justice cannot sleep forever."

On May 8, 1859, John Brown, one of the leaders of the Free-Soil movement, proclaimed a provisional constitution for the United States and rose in arms denouncing slavery as the most flagrant violation of the eternal and self-evident truths proclaimed by the Declaration of Independence. He intrenched himself at Harper's Ferry against the Virginia militia. He was wounded, taken prisoner, tried and executed.

During the Civil War, the Union soldiers marched to the front singing: "John Brown's body lies mouldering in the grave, but his soul goes marching on."

On February 27, 1860, Lincoln, from the platform at Cooper Union, delivered the most scathing condemnation of the abominable institution of slavery. According to Henry C. Whitney, Lincoln's friend and biographer, that speech "was a massive structure of *unhewn* logic, without an *interstice* or flaw. It was a dignified, stately, solemn declaration of the concrete principles of liberty as they existed in the minds of the

American people."

On January 1, 1863, the document now celebrated in the annals of humanity was proclaimed:

"I, Abraham Lincoln, President of the United States, by virtue of the power in me vested as Commander-in-Chief of the Army and Navy of the United States in time of actual armed rebellion against the authority and Government of the United States, do order and declare . . . .

". . . That all persons held as slaves . . . are and henceforward shall be free. . . .

". . . And upon this act, sincerely believed to be an act of justice, warranted by the Constitution, upon military necessity, I invoke the considerate judgment of mankind and the gracious favor of Almighty God."

Thus was slavery abolished in the United States, and the hope that the very last vestige of slavery would one day disappear from the face of the earth gathered strength in the consciousness of man.

That noteworthy event stimulated the efforts of Brazilian abolitionists and made the position of their opponents precarious.

The problem of slavery became a social and moral issue that gripped the consciousness of the whole nation. Since 1831 the importation of new slaves had been officially forbidden. In reality that drastic measure had been in effect as far back as 1810, by the terms of a treaty with England.

The Emperor, Dom Pedro II, who, after a regency lasting ten years, had been solemnly crowned at the age of fifteen (July 18, 1841) was a resolute foe of slavery and an ardent abolitionist. The Emperor had a better than average mind; he was a man of noble sentiments and liberal ideas. There is no doubt that he felt his situation keenly. Stephan Zweig said that it was exceedingly painful for this highly cultured man, on his trips to Europe, to feel that the most eminent representatives of humanity, to whose friendship he aspired—men such as Pasteur, Charcot, Lamartine, Victor Hugo, Wagner and Nietzsche—looked on him as the monarch ruling the only empire which still tolerated the flogging and branding of slaves.

However, Dom Pedro II was unable to make his moral convictions, his feeling of repulsion for slavery, the law of his empire. For more than forty years his anti-slavery opinions, expressed with great warmth, were blocked by the stone wall of vested interests, although his sentiments were shared by many Brazilian statesmen, among them the prominent Vizconde de Río Branco. In 1871, Brazil passed a law freeing every child born to a female slave. Nevertheless, the problem of slavery in Brazil still was far from a final solution. The law was disregarded on remote plantations, and the slave traders continued to ply their business on a large scale.

It took almost two decades more for full and effective abolition to become a reality. Finally there arose a valiant champion of freedom, Joaquín Nabuco, who eventually was to win a complete victory in the fight against slavery. A mulatto journalist, José de Patrocinio, and a negro lawyer and former slave, Luis Gama, assisted him in his unremitting efforts, the former in the press and the latter in the courts.

Nabuco was famous as a poet and writer before being elected to Congress. James Daroy wrote that the most touching feature about this gifted man was that, for all his greatness, he had such unpretentious simplicity, and that so brilliant an intellect had so warm a heart.

It was that warm heart of his that soon led him into politics, the better to serve the cause of liberation of the slaves, whose condition had moved him deeply and for whose freedom henceforth he devoted all his boundless energy. In 1879 he told the other members of Congress, "A liberal may not delay, not even for a single moment, the great day of emancipation."

In 1880, to the Government's great dismay, Nabuco submitted to Congress a bill for liberation that was to produce strong repercussions throughout the nation. Undiscouraged by his failure to be reelected in 1891, he became the London correspondent of the *Jornal do Commercio,* and in its columns he explained to his countrymen the reasons for his anti-slavery campaign:

"It was no thought-out plan which led me to combat slavery, but rather because it was incompatible with my own moral nature. I have acted thus in response to what I feel to be the only patriotism worthy the name: that of a Brazilian anxious to acknowledge his country without blushing for shame. 'Slavery' is a word that may have lost all meaning in some minds, but to others it is like a branding iron that sears the forehead with the mark of degradation."

Nabuco's popularity grew enormously, and on his return from London he was overwhelmingly reelected to Congress. Little by little, his untiring and varied activities began to yield results. In 1884, Providencia de Ceará and in 1885 the Amazonas abolished slavery in their respective territories. Many owners set their slaves free. In 1886 a provisional law provided for the liberation of every slave over sixty. Finally, May 13, 1888, the long awaited statute abolishing slavery was passed. It provided for the immediate emancipation of all slaves throughout Brazil. This law "to which the name 'golden' was given later, was truly the crowning glory of a great statesman, and will keep his memory alive forever in the history of the nation and in the gratitude of the race thus freed."

The peoples of the United States and Brazil had been equally slow in completing the task of abolition. They had, however, reached the same goal by different ways. The United States achieved abolition earlier, but only at the cost of a bloody and long-drawn-out civil war. In Brazil the same result was not attained until 1888, but there it was by peaceful means, through a series of legal enactments.

Few happenings in the history of Brazil offer more eloquent proof of her conciliatory spirit that shuns violence if persuasion can be used. When the campaign began in favor of the bill decreeing the freedom of every child born to a slave, Vizconde de Río Branco, the Premier of the Imperial Cabinet and the father of the no less worthy and perhaps better known Barón de Río Branco, carried on a spirited parliamentary debate in defense of his proposal. When, after stormy meetings in which the eloquence of the eminent statesman overrode the opposition, the Senate finally passed the law, a wild burst of enthusiasm swept the crowd waiting outside, and when Río Branco appeared he was received with shouts of delight, a wild and interminable ovation, and flowers were showered on his head.

The Minister of the United States picked up some of the

blossoms strewn upon the pavement, as a souvenir, he said, of what Brazil had paid for a change that had cost his own country rivers of blood.

The vast area of Brazil, except, of course, the unexplored regions and the extensive *donaterías* (grants), required a great deal of labor for development; so did the mines of gold and precious stones which were soon discovered, and the cutting of Brazil-wood, the colony's main source of wealth. The colonial government, to obtain men for these operations, first organized the *entradas,* later the *bandeiras.*

The *entradas* were expeditions designed to reduce the Indians to slavery. By trickery and gifts of clothing, beads and firewater, they seized the inhabitants of whole villages and enslaved them, separating parents and children, brothers and sisters, husbands and wives, and distributing them among the captain, the army and the *donatarios* (grantees), or else selling them as slaves to whomever needed them.

The *bandeiras* in the south, mainly São Paulo, also were organized to hunt down Indians and discover mines. The word *bandeirante* (according to Duque de Estrada) is derived from *bandeira,* a band commanded by a chieftain. Brazil had her *bandeirantes,* "just as Greece had her *banditti,* of whom Jupiter, the Father of the Gods, was the supreme chief."

A *bandeira* consisted of six hundred men led by a troop commander with two captains as aides. They went on forays through the Indian regions, following the same tactics as the *entradas.* To expedite matters, if the inhabitants showed any resistance, the village was burned down to force them into the open so they might be caught more easily. Prisoners were yoked together with chains and iron collars in groups of forty and taken by water or overland for interminable distances.

It is not hard to imagine what kind of outrages the *bandeirantes* committed on their expeditions, which were fraught with all the dangers and hardships of traversing impenetrable forests crossed by enormous rivers and abounding in wild animals and poisonous snakes, where the menace of disease and innumerable privations was ever lurking.

This general outline of the conditions of the masses in colonial days applies more or less accurately to the other countries of the Americas, especially those with large aboriginal populations, such as Central America, Peru, Colombia and Bolivia. Everywhere, the cruelest exploitation of man by man held sway.

The conquering minorities succeeded in keeping the aboriginal masses in ignorance and slavery. It was not deemed advisable to promote education in Spanish America, the inhabitants of which were destined "by nature" to labor and die in the depths of the mines. At a solemn meeting, the Consular Tribunal at Mexico declared that the Indians were a brutish, vicious and ignorant race, mere automatons unworthy either of acting as representatives or of being represented.

Of course the natives, deprived of all education except such rudimentary teaching as the missionaries could give, were never able to hold public office or employment, military rank, or high positions in the Church or courts. It is true that there were in Spain's American possessions Indians who did excel when, by rare chance, they were afforded an opportunity. Schools, universities and seminaries were established in many cities, but the great body of the Indians remained sunk in ignorance by the deliberate decision of their conquerors.

The colonies also were subject to innumerable restrictions that prevented the free flow of trade and industry. Certain crops, such as the grape and olive, tobacco and sugar cane, were limited to specified provinces and intended only for local consumption. Everything else was imported from the Spanish Peninsula where the *Casa de Contratación,* or Colonial Trade Commission, at Seville was the sole body authorized to engage in commerce with the colonies, except such trade as was carried on with Asia via Manila and Acapulco.

European Spaniards were wont to say that Spanish America should always be joined to Spain, whatever the fate of the Peninsula might be, and the last surviving Spaniard was entitled to rule over the Americans.

The arrogance of the conquerors and their ingrained conviction that they were superior beings were the reasons for the countless exactions imposed on the conquered.

That eminent and much attacked defender of the Indians, Bartolomé de las Casas, in appealing to the Spanish Crown to put a stop to the depopulation of the West Indies, declared, "If I were to relate to Your Majesty the cruelty of the Spaniards to the Indians, your Majesty's entrails would be wrung with grief."

All the circumstances described above—which should not be forgotten by those who attempt in the name of Hispanism to divide the Americas by stressing only the iniquities of the Anglo-Saxons—are not traits peculiar and exclusive to the Spanish and Portuguese *conquistadores,* but are inherent in all violent conquest and in every attempt at domination. A conquered country is booty to be divided up, and man himself is part of the booty.

Therefore, all these gloomy considerations on colonial days are not specific charges against Spain. They are an indictment of the aggression against other peoples which the strong have practiced throughout history. There is a world of truth in Quintana's ringing words: "They are crimes of the epoch, not of Spain."

From colonial servitude sprang those creole and mestizo elements which were to produce the champions of the independence of the American nations: Hidalgo, Bolívar, San Martín, Sucre. When the independence of all these countries was proclaimed, they all shared in the beautiful illusion that the freedom and happiness of the peoples would enter for all time through the triumphal arches under which their leaders rode. But a long path still had to be traveled. New forms of servitude and of abuse of power, which we shall take up in the pages to follow, were to replace the old.

T *Colonial Servitude* · II

THE DIRECT SUBJECTION OF MAN BY MAN throughout history has assumed forms as heartrending, ruthless and detestable as the trade in slaves and their exploitation which we have just described.

In colonial times the condition of the masses over a vast area of the American Continent dominated by Spain and Portugal was not so very different from real slavery.

The determination of the *conquistadores* to reduce the Indians to slavery, in the full sense of the word, was strong and persistent. That they failed to do so, even though canonists and other jurists declared slavery legal under international and civil law, was because both Popes and Kings firmly opposed it and never gave their consent.

Paul III, that iron-willed Pontiff who was a resolute defender of the freedom of the Indians in the Americas, addressed a *pastorale officium* to the Cardinal Archbishop of Toledo on May 29, 1537, expressly and positively prohibiting the reduction of Indians to slavery, under pain of full excommunication.

The displeasure shown by their Catholic Majesties at grants of Indian prisoners made by Columbus to certain of his friends and sponsors, after a bloody battle, was a matter of common knowledge. The Queen ordered that the Indians be restored to their natural condition at Columbus' expense. After that, Fernando ordered that no one was to bring any aborigines from their own lands to Europe, even with their consent. But as a matter of fact, the discoverers and conquerors of the Americas deemed themselves justified in resisting the King himself in the defense of their alleged rights. The cost of discovery and conquest, with the exception of Columbus' first expedition, had been defrayed out of their own pockets. Motivated by greed, or their adventurous spirit, or to escape the hand of the law, they had accomplished everything by their own efforts, running severe risks and suffering great hardships.

Cortez and Diego Velázquez, the Governor of Cuba, joined forces in a purely mercantile venture, safeguarded by certain articles or contracts, to finance the expedition against the mainland. Similarly Pizarro, Almagro and Luque signed a deed of partnership for the conquest of new lands at Panama on March 10, 1526. Each was to contribute money, arms or his own effort to the undertaking, thus giving their private venture definitely a business character.

So it is not surprising that the status of free vassals accorded the Indians by the Crown proved to be an empty, meaningless right when confronted by the greed of the conquerors. Despite severe threats from the Crown and the efforts of the religious orders and of some few authorities, the aborigines still were harshly treated by their overlords. As the Russian moujik said, "God is high in His heaven and the Czar is very far away."

Columbus proceeded to distribute the recently discovered and conquered lands among his companions as authorized by the Royal Ordinance of June 22, 1497, in turn derived from the bull of the Spanish Pope, Alexander VI, issued May 3, 1493, which had awarded to their Catholic Majesties "any lands discovered or that might be discovered by their command." The Royal Ordinance spoke of lands, not inhabitants, but of course the conquerors, who had passed from the lowest social rank in Spain to that of great lords in the colonies, scorned to till the soil themselves. "To keep on being diggers, we need not have crossed the ocean," they said, maintaining that the lands were of no use if they had no one to cultivate them. Hence Columbus, on his authority, allotted to each colonist a number of Indians who thereby were reduced to the condition of serfs.

But as there were not enough natives in Hispaniola, the Spaniards sent out expeditions to nearby islands to hunt down Indians, thus initiating a slave trade which soon became the form of piracy which earned such a sinister reputation for the inhabitants of Hispaniola of those days.

The methods of allotment learned in Cuba were introduced by Cortez into New Spain, where they spread so rapidly that on the belated arrival of the Royal Ordinances prohibiting them, he informed the King in a letter dated October 15, 1524, that there was no other way of settling the Spaniards on the land and rewarding their services except by grants of Indians.

Thus the aboriginal population was converted into a vast herd subdivided into groups of different sizes. This human herd was looked upon by the settlers as capital, in some cases all they had. As these allotments were for the lifetime of the original holder, he endeavored by all means, fair or foul, usually the latter, to squeeze from both land and Indian the fullest measure of profit.

Nicolás de Ovando came out in 1502 as the bearer of instructions from the Crown to the effect that the aborigines were to be considered free vassals of the King. No labor or service of any kind was to be exacted from them without their consent or proper remuneration. But obedience to the Crown was not one of the outstanding virtues of the colonizers of those days.

The condition of the Indians was so pitiable that it gave rise to the Royal Order of 1526, a scathing indictment of the rapacious colonists and a dismal picture of the bloody horrors that defaced the royal domain in the Americas: "Don Carlos, by the grace of God the ever august Emperor, and Donna Juana his mother by the same grace of God, the King and Queen of Castile, León, Arragón, etc.; inasmuch as we have testimony of, and it is notorious, that the unbridled greed of some of our subjects, who have crossed to our territories beyond the sea, by the ill-treatment they have meted out to the native Indians of said territories, not only through the enormous and excessive toil laid upon them by keeping them in the mines to take out gold and in the pearl fisheries and other labor and gainful ventures, forcing them to work excessively and inordinately but without furnishing either clothing or food to sustain life, treating them with cruelty and hostility far worse than if they were slaves, . . . "

The formula of the *encomienda* or allotment which modified the *repartimiento* or grant, despite the fact that the real situation continued to be the same or worse, read: "To you John Doe we entrust so many Indians, the subjects of such-and-such a chief so that you may teach them the matters of our holy Catholic faith." As will be seen, nothing was said about the personal and compulsory servitude of the Indian, yet under the abuses his condition of life became worse than outright slavery.

"The allotment of the Indians in *encomiendas* to the Spaniards just after the Conquest," said the Venezuelan sociologist, Julio C. Salas, "was a form of servitude much harsher than actual slavery for the natives were obliged to render constant service to their *encomenderos* or masters for an unlimited period. Although the duration of the *encomienda* was restricted to two or three lifetimes, when the time expired the Indians became the property of the King; and the latter nearly always allotted them again or gave them to his courtiers or favorites, who sent out agents or overseers from Europe to manage their estates."

But there was something perhaps even worse than what I have described, that lasted well into the nineteenth century, especially in Peru. This was the *mita,* or selection by lot among the native inhabitants of a given region to do forced labor, especially in mines belonging to Spaniards. These conscripts were known as *mitayos.* Under this system the actual position of the Indian laborer was very like that of a slave.

Chile was a colony which, because of special conditions that existed there and the invincible resistance of the Araucanians, remained free to a large extent from the calamities the Conquest unleashed on the Americas. Even so, in 1844, Don José María Lastarria, in a memorial to the University of Chile, wrote, "On these unfortunate Americans were imposed duties contrary to their customs, their beliefs and even their most-cherished inclinations, until they were finally subjected to the heaviest labor and the most shameful slavery." He concluded by asking, "Where shall we seek today the vast empire of the Incas with its six million vassals?"

The Guaraní Indians in the Argentine were victims of the same system of the *encomiendas.* And in the enormous territory of Brazil—more than five million square miles—conquered by Portugal, a very similar procedure was followed. The *donaterías,* resembling the *encomiendas,* were established. The only difference was that the *donaterías* were much larger.

B *The Monroe Doctrine* · III

Y THE BEGINNING OF THE NINETEENTH CENTURY fundamental changes in the doctrine of Public Law had taken place, not only in the Americas but in Europe as well. Revolutionary ideas had been spread in many countries by the soldiers of Napoleon and had struck roots in the peoples, who called upon their rulers to give them reforms similar to those introduced in France, to restrict the absolute power of monarchs.

With the fervor of this new civic zeal, the long drawn-out fight between liberalism and absolutism began, the peoples demanding constitution and parliament, and the monarchs stubbornly intent on preserving intact the privileges of the *ancien régime.*

From time to time the aspirations of the people asserted themselves with violence, and the despots found it necessary to set up an international organization for repression. To this end the Holy Alliance came into being at the Congresses of Vienna (1815) and Aix-la-Chapelle (1818). It took the form of a pentarchy—Russia, Prussia, Austria, France and England. The members of this coalition, while doing lip-service to a system of government professing the principles of the Christian religion, in reality had no other aim than to crush by blood and iron every movement against despotism.

Whenever disquieting symptoms were observed in any of the European countries, the rulers met and decided among themselves the best way of defending the throne that was in danger. In this way various Congresses took place one after the other —at Vienna and Carlsbad in 1819 and 1820, at Troppau and Lañbach in 1820 and 1821, and at Verona in 1822.

At Verona the matters under consideration dealt almost entirely with Spanish affairs—those of peninsular Spain and what was left of Spain's overseas colonies.

Since the Aix-la-Chapelle Congress, Ferdinand VII had applied for military assistance from his allies, not only to return to that absolutism the Constitution of Cádiz had assailed, but also to reduce his rebellious American colonies to submission. The Czar of Russia warmly seconded the Spanish sovereign's plans, and even contributed ships for a large punitive expedition that was to have sailed from Cádiz early in 1820.

The King of Spain, in the eyes of legitimist Europe, was the rightful sovereign of the geographically more important areas of the New World. His title of Emperor of the Indies represented a right which, although challenged by a strong minority, was still respected by a large section of the population of Spanish America. So much was this the case that at the outset of the Spanish colonies' struggle for independence, nothing was said about separation from the mother country, but only of preserving the rights of the Spanish crown, which had been jeopardized by the French invasion of the Peninsula.

At the northern tip of the American Continent, the Czar

of Russia was the lord of vast territories whose boundaries extended somewhat vaguely from Alaska down to the coast of California. In 1812, Barov, that Russian Governor whose aggressive policies had won for him the nickname of the "Little Czar," succeeded in establishing a colony not far from Bodega Bay, only 30 miles north of San Francisco.

Several years after the Congress of Vienna, the minister of Louis XVIII at Washington, Hyde de Neuville, sent Cardinal Richelieu a plan for the establishment of one or more monarchies in South America, the thrones to be occupied by princes of the House of Bourbon. The French Minister said he hoped to obtain the acquiescence of the United States in carrying out that plan, in exchange for France's good offices in the cession of the Floridas.

The King of Spain, after his unsuccessful attempt to win the aid of the powers assembled at the Congress of Aix-la-Chapelle, found himself impotent to carry into effect his schemes for the recovery of his former colonies. All the resources of his kingdom had been expended in fitting out a great expeditionary force, which all through 1819 waited in vain off León Island near Cádiz for the necessary transports.

Meanwhile, Chateaubriand, the Minister of Foreign Affairs of France, statesman, and poet, had indulged in dreams of extending French control, by then firmly established in Spain, to her overseas colonies. He laid before Ferdinand VII an agreement, which Russia viewed with favor, by which the colonies of Latin America were to be transformed into a league of principalities with a Bourbon prince at the head of each one. These princes would be chosen from the French, Spanish and Italian branches of the family. The system thus founded was to be guaranteed by the members of the Holy Alliance.

But England, without whose cooperation any overseas action was out of the question, declared herself emphatically in favor of the liberty of the Americas. England's Foreign Minister, Lord Castlereagh, flatly stated that his government would not participate in any adventure sponsored by the Holy Alliance, aimed at restoring the newborn American Republics to Spanish domination.

This was the situation as the Congress of Verona assembled,

without Castlereagh's presence; he had killed himself on the eve of his departure for Verona. Though the five-power alliance still nominally existed, it had been shaken to its foundation. The most pressing business was to put down the rebellion of the Spanish people led by Riego against Ferdinand VII because of the monarch's disavowal of the Constitution of Cádiz, which he had sworn to uphold. To this end the powers agreed to send a French army, commanded by the Duc d'Angoulême, to the Peninsula. The expedition was victorious and achieved its purpose. It spread death and ruin through the Spanish nation, and upheld the ancient despotism of the throne.

On August 22, 1823, George Canning, the new British Foreign Minister, with an eye to England's influence and trade with Spain's former colonies, clearly outlined his country's position to Richard Rush, the United States Minister to Great Britain. He wanted to see if an agreement between the two Anglo-Saxon nations could be concluded *vis-a-vis* Latin America, along the following lines:

"1. We conceive the recovery of the colonies of Spain to be hopeless.

"2. We conceive . . . the recognition of them, as independent states, to be one of time and circumstances.

"3. We are, however, by no means disposed to throw any impediment in the way of an arrangement between them and the mother country by amicable negotiation.

"4. We aim not at the possession of any portion of them ourselves.

"5. We could not see any portion of them transferred to any other power with indifference."

President Monroe thought that the importance of the invitation thus extended warranted his asking the author of the Declaration of Independence, Thomas Jefferson, for advice, and wrote requesting his opinion.

Jefferson received the inquiry at his Monticello retreat in 1823. His answer is one of the historical documents that have influenced most strongly the destinies of the Americas:

"The question presented by the letters you have sent me is the most momentous which has ever been offered to my contemplation since that of Independence. That made us a nation, this sets our compass and points the course which we are to steer through the ocean of time opening on us. And never could we embark on it under circumstances more auspicious. Our first and fundamental maxim should be, never to entangle ourselves in the broils of Europe; our second, never to suffer Europe to intermeddle with cis-Atlantic affairs. America, North and South, has a set of interests distinct from those of Europe, and peculiarly her own. She should therefore have a system of her own, separate and apart from that of Europe. While the last is laboring to become the domicile of despotism, our endeavor should surely be, to make our hemisphere that of freedom.

"One nation, most of all, could disturb us in this pursuit; she now offers to lead, aid, and accompany us in it. By acceding to her proposition, we detach her from the bands, bring her mighty weight into the scale of free government, and emancipate a continent at one stroke, which might otherwise linger long in doubt and difficulty. Great Britain is the nation which can do us the most harm of any one, of all on earth; and with her on our side we need not fear the whole world. With her, then, we should most sedulously cherish a cordial friendship; and nothing would tend to knit our affections than to be fighting once more, side by side, in the same cause. Not that I would purchase even her amity at the price of taking part in her wars.

"But the war in which the present proposition might engage us, should that be its consequence, is not her war, but ours. Its object is to introduce and establish the American system, of keeping out of our land all foreign powers, of never permitting those of Europe to intermeddle with the affairs of our nation. It is to maintain our own principle, not to depart from it. And if, to facilitate this, we can effect a division in the body of the European powers, and draw over to our side its most powerful member, surely we should do it. But I am clearly of Mr. Canning's opinion, that it will prevent instead of provoking war. With Great Britain withdrawn from their scale and shifted into that of our two continents, all Europe combined would not undertake such a war, for how would they propose to get at either enemy without superior fleets? Nor is the occasion to be slighted which this proposition offers of declaring our protest against the atrocious violations of the rights of nations by the interference of any one in the internal affairs of another, so flagitiously begun by Bonaparte, and now continued by the equally lawless Alliance calling itself Holy."

In the spirit of these ideas, Monroe in his message of December 2 of that same year, proclaimed the celebrated doctrine that bears his name.

The essential paragraphs of that message are those which consider as principles of international law with which the rights and interests of the United States are closely bound up, "that the American Continents, by the free and independent condition which they have assumed and maintain, are henceforth not to be considered as subjects for future colonization by any European powers;" the declaration, as a national duty, that "we owe it, therefore, to candor and to the amicable relations existing between the United States and those [European] powers, to declare that we should consider any attempt on their part to extend their system to any portion of this hemisphere as dangerous to our peace and safety." And as a consequence —it is asserted further on—"we could not view any interposition for the purpose of oppressing them, or controlling in any other manner their destiny, by any European power, in any other light than as the manifestation of an unfriendly disposition towards the United States."

Lastly, Monroe made this forceful statement: "It is impossible that the allied powers should extend their political system to any portion of either continent without endangering our peace and happiness; nor can anyone believe that our southern brethren, if left to themselves, would adopt it of their own accord. It is equally impossible, therefore, that we should behold such interposition, in any form, with indifference."

This doctrine, like the utterances of the Delphic oracle, has received the most contradictory interpretations. There are, however, two facts that clearly and undeniably owe their origin to Monroe's pronouncement. One is the enormous service rendered to the independent nations of the Americas by a policy that safeguarded them from the conspiracies and greed of the European powers looking to renewed attempts at colonization. The other is that, on the strength of this doctrine, powerful business interests developed in a few decades the system known as American Imperialism.

The Doctrine of the Americas · IV

THE ANTECEDENTS OF THE MONROE DOCTRINE, its original sources, such as Canning's proposition, President Monroe's consultation, Jefferson's letter in reply, and the President's message of December 2, 1823, all explain how the idea of publicly supporting the independence, sovereignty and free systems of the American nations arose and took shape in the mind of the author of the Doctrine. Let us disregard the distortions—"Manifest Destiny," "the Olney Postulate," "Dollar Diplomacy," "the Big Stick Policy"—to which the Doctrine was subjected.

The three main principles set forth in President Monroe's message that have given birth to the Monroe Doctrine are: That the states of the New World have acquired the right to independence; that the United States will oppose any attempt at renewed European colonization in the Americas; and that it will also repel any form whatsoever of European intervention on this Continent. Although when enunciated, these principles, as all America has held, signified only an international policy for which the United States was wholly responsible, they embraced a doctrine which in its essentials—no intervention, and protection of the Western Hemisphere—has at all times had the support of all Latin America ever since the beginning of its fight for liberty.

Indisputable evidence of this may be found in many documents of the period. Opinions of contemporary Latin American leaders (taken from the comprehensive compilation made by Planas Suárez, the authority on international affairs, in his series of lectures some years ago in the Academy of International Law at The Hague), reflect the spirit of the times:

Francisco de Miranda, the illustrious Venezuelan who even before Bolívar had raised the standard of South American independence, declared that the time had come to inaugurate a new America, united by common interest in a vast brotherhood. He iterates this in a letter to the Captain General and Council of Havana, September 10, 1797; in a document drawn up at Paris under his direction, in 1795, which contained the draft for an alliance between Latin America and the United States; and in his celebrated manifesto of the same period, inspired by the victory over England of her northern colonies.

Juan Egaña, in his "Project for a Declaration of Rights of the Chilean People," published in 1810, asserted the urgent need of uniting the peoples of America to insure peace and quiet both at home and abroad. He added words which at that time seemed very daring:

"It is very hard for each people to maintain, even in the face of serious danger, its own isolated sovereignty. . . . When the Americas, assembled in Congress, shall speak to the rest of the world, on that day their voice will be respected and it will not be easy to oppose their resolutions."

Bernardo O'Higgins pointed out to the Chileans, in 1818, the "desirability of constituting a Latin Confederation of the Americas to defend their civil and political liberties." Juan José San Martín, in an address to the Argentine people, proclaimed the need of achieving "a close union of the countries of South America to guarantee their aspirations for freedom and independence."

Bernardo Monteagudo, who had also played an important part in the liberation of the River Plate Republic, announced that the New World would in the future constitute one big family.

José Artigas, in certain "Ordinances Relative to Privateering," laid down the fundamental principles of collective defense in words that sound like a brilliant forecast of contemporary decisions: "Every act involving a menace of subjection or fresh conquest of the River Plate provinces or of any others whatsoever on the American Continent shall be considered a hostile act."

Mariano Montillo, Venezuelan general, told the Commander-in-Chief of the Spanish Army, Pablo Morillo, shortly before the latter returned to Spain, that he would never consent to any negotiations unless the independence of the Americas was first recognized.

José Cecilio de Valle, an illustrious Central American, in a "Project for a League of the American Nations," drafted before Monroe's Declaration, outlined a plan to prevent any American nation from falling a prey to foreign invaders.

Manuel Torres, who was sent by Bolívar to represent Greater Colombia before the Washington Government, in a note addressed to the Secretary of State, John Quincy Adams, November 30, 1821, in which he applied for recognition of the Republic of Colombia, urged the President of the United States to draft an American pact to protect our republican institutions against the Holy Alliance.

To the foregoing eloquent examples I shall add another by the initiator of Mexican independence, Father Hidalgo, which appears in a study recently published by Alfonso García Robles. Hidalgo's manifesto of January 12, 1811, explained to the people of what was still a Spanish Viceroyalty the reasons for the liberating movement he headed. Addressing himself not only to the Mexicans but to all other Americans as well, Hidalgo told them that "the day of the glory and of the public happiness of this America" had arrived.

Already a month previous, December 15, 1810, Hidalgo had published a manifesto in a similar vein intended to answer the charges brought against him by the Inquisition. Appealing repeatedly to the Americans for unity, in language suited to times of war, he said: "Let us unite, then, all of us who were born on this fortunate soil. Let us look upon all those who are not American as aliens and enemies of our rights." Morelos, another Mexican leader, in a "brief argument" addressed to the nation on November 2, 1813, spoke in similar terms, warning Europeans that Americans were already free "by the grace of God."

Fittingly to complete and summarize the foregoing thoughts we cannot do better than reproduce a few paragraphs—either from personal letters or from the various international instruments drafted in connection with the Panama Congress—that reflect the doctrine of Bolívar, since undoubtedly he above all possessed the most profound and complete concept of the interdependence of the destinies of the American Republics and the need for close continental solidarity. In a manuscript dated 1818, the Liberator asserted that "the New World should be constituted by free and independent nations, united among themselves by a body of law common to all of them, to govern their foreign relations. Differences of origin and color would lose their influence and force. The strength of all these nations would come to the aid of any single one having to face a foreign enemy." And in his general invitation to the Panama Congress, dated at Lima, December 7, 1824, after explaining the aims of the proposed assembly designed to provide permanent foundations for the common interests and relations of the American Republics, he concluded:

"The day our plenipotentiaries make the exchanges of their powers will stamp in the diplomatic history of the world an immortal epoch.

When, after a hundred centuries, posterity shall search for the origin of our public law, and shall remember the compacts —that solidified its destiny, they will finger with respect the protocols of the Isthmus. In them they will find the plan of the first alliances that shall sketch the mark of our relations with the universe. What, then, shall be the Isthmus of Corinth compared with that of Panama?

In reply to Bolívar's circular, the Colombian Government, March 6, 1825, through its Secretary of Foreign Affairs, Francisco de P. Santander, called upon all the American peoples to adopt political pacts that would crush any attempt at intervention by the European powers menacing the sovereign rights of the American peoples.

The "Treaty of Perpetual Union, League and Confederation" concluded at the Panama Congress July 15, 1826, provides in article 2 that:

"The object of this perpetual compact will be to maintain in common, defensively and offensively, should occasion arise, the sovereignty and independence of all and each of the confederated powers of America against foreign subjection."

The testimony here reproduced—further examples would only be superfluous—clearly proves the Latin American origin of the essential premise of the Monroe Doctrine, the defense of the New World.

This is the reason all Latin American internationalists have been unanimous in proclaiming that origin, and several prominent writers in the United States have shared the same opinion.

Dema Skinner, in an essay published in 1923 on the first centennial of the Monroe Doctrine, entitled *One Century of the Monroe Doctrine,* asserted that the most notable of the discoveries which would profoundly alter generally accepted ideas of the Doctrine was that relating to its origin. Most people believe that it was conceived by North American statesmen with the approval and assistance of Canning, the British Foreign Minister, but Skinner adds, "it is an undeniable historical fact that the idea was almost entirely of South

American origin. . . ."

John B. Whitton, a professor at Princeton University, endorsing the studies of Planas Suárez, Baltasar Brum and Alejandro Alvarez, concurs in the opinion that the American principles contained in the Monroe Doctrine are continentally inspired, that Monroe did nothing more than echo the feelings of all Latin America.

T *Shades of Bolivar and Monroe* · V

HE PASSAGE OF TIME SHOULD TRANSFORM THE unilateral character of the Monroe Doctrine into the solidarity of a continental dogma. As a matter of fact, Latin America, on its side, also felt the urgent need to defend itself against the threatened aggression by European powers. Thus it was that the notion of Pan Americanism was born in the mind, not only of Bolívar, but of many other American leaders. When the peoples pondered on the advantages of a united front and realized the numerous dangers of isolation, then the spiritual value of that historic ideal, the union of all the peoples of America, stood out pure in splendid relief.

The Latin American doctrine of the unity of the Americas is much broader in scope than the Monroe Doctrine. Although the independent leaders of Spain's former colonies always stressed and promoted union among the new Latin American states, never for a single minute did they lose sight of the necessity that this union should embrace all the peoples of the Continent, including the United States.

It is opportune to state that Canada also should consider herself an integral part of our Continental Union, which undoubtedly will be strengthened on the day it receives the spiritual and democratic contribution of that great people.

The explanation for the wider outlook of the Latin Americans is that Madrid's old colonies were the only ones still actually fighting for their freedom and consequently were the ones most directly menaced by a common danger, whereas the United States had shaken off the tutelage of the mother country several decades before.

Convincing proofs of this are to be found in the deliberations of the Panama Congress in 1826. Even though the United States was not represented, its absence was due only to the obstacles raised by the Congress at Washington against participation in the conference. The result was that the delegation from the United States, whose appointment had been ratified too late, failed to reach the Isthmian city in time.

As an Argentinian writer, Sáenz Peña, has aptly stated: "The Panama Congress harbored no hostile intentions toward the United States, which had from the beginning been invited to participate, nor against the Monroe Doctrine. On the contrary, it was inspired by the wish to bestow on that Doctrine continental scope and significance, through the conscious and free adherence of the new nationalities."

It must also be borne in mind that the ideas so warmly expressed by eminent Latin Americans were shared by many public men in the United States.

Four years before, Henry Clay, Speaker of the House of Representatives, expressed sentiments identical to those which animated other friends of liberty in the North. In a speech before the House he recommended the institution of "a human-freedom league in America," in which "all the nations from Hudson's Bay to Cape Horn," should be united.

And it was Clay who, in his instructions as Secretary of State to the United States Delegation to the Panama Congress, expressed exactly the same sentiments as Bolívar regarding the importance of a Congress at Panama.

This fervor for the achievement of a Continental Union sank deep into the spirit of John Quincy Adams, then President of the United States. He pointed out to Congress that perhaps "in the lapse of many Centuries" no other "opportunity so favourable" would be presented to the Government of the United States "to subserve the benevolent purposes of Divine Providence, to dispense the promised blessings of the Redeemer of Mankind; as will now be placed in their power, by participating in the deliberations of the Panama Congress."

And yet slavery continued to be an officially recognized institution in the American Union. Spanish America, on the other hand, had come out flatly against slavery, and abolished it by proclamation, with two exceptions: Cuba, still a Spanish colony, where servitude continued to exist, and Brazil, where it also survived until 1888. Also, it was proposed that the Panama Congress recognize Haiti as a nation. The slaves there had rebelled against their masters and established their independence. Consequently the pro-slavery Southern States of the American Union did not look with kindly eyes on a Congress that was to concern itself with the recognition of Haitian independence, even if the new-born State would not likely be represented at the Assembly.

These were the fundamental reasons why, although President Adams and Secretary Clay finally won from the Senate the ratification of the appointments of the delegates, the ratification came so late that the delegation was unable to attend the Panama Congress.

After this patent failure, it was not until late in the last century that the First Inter-American Conference of American Nations, held at Washington, from October 2, 1889, to April 19, 1890, gave expression to renewed efforts for continental cooperation by the establishment of the Pan-American Union.

In the circular note sent out by Secretary of State James G. Blaine to the governments of the American nations, inviting them to participate in a general Inter-American Congress at Washington in 1882—which for various reasons never met—the Secretary stressed that the United States would take part in the conference on the same footing as the other countries represented and as "a single member among many co-ordinated and co-equal states."

Unfortunately these noble words were followed by an immediate contradiction in the behavior of the United States in its inter-American relations. It is enough to recall that right after these declarations, American imperialism developed with great swiftness. The very rapidity of this development and the acts to which it gave rise, created for the pristine Monroe Doctrine an atmosphere of such distrust that the ideal of Pan-American unity was pushed far aside. The times were not yet ripe for such a notion as solidarity, which found itself confronted by an economic system that backed up commercial relations with force, and which did not correspond to the deficient means of communication between the peoples or to the anti-democratic international realities of those days.

The world was dominated, especially in the international sphere, by the greed for profits of large investors and trusts. These excluded from their financial calculations all consideration of future needs and the ethical values of civilization.

However, that which Panama failed to achieve, and that which lacked vitality and enthusiasm in 1889, became a reality when, after the last World War, the menace of a fresh conflagration began to darken the horizon. This menace carried home the conviction that it was more urgent than ever to tighten the bonds of American solidarity, to ensure the survival of free institutions and the defense of the Continent.

These sentiments of substantial understanding and agreement between the peoples of the Americas manifested themselves clearly and frankly in the policy known as that of the Good Neighbor, proclaimed by President Roosevelt in his inaugural speech on March 4, 1933, as well as in an address delivered at the Woodrow Wilson Foundation in December of the same year. In it Mr. Roosevelt vigorously ratified his doctrine, as he did in his speech to Congress in January, 1934, and in another delivered at Cartagena, Colombia, in July, 1934. This frank and cordial attitude has been reiterated by a number of statesmen in the Northern Republic, men of such standing as Vice-President Henry A. Wallace, Secretary of State Cordell Hull and Under-Secretary Welles.

The Sixth Pan-American Conference, held in Havana in 1928, was unable to reach satisfactory agreements on the non-intervention problem, for intervention was the keystone of a tragic interpretation of the Monroe Doctrine. The Mexican Foreign Office, before the Seventh International American Congress at Montevideo in 1933, frankly and clearly discussed the problem of the interpretation of the Monroe Doctrine and proposed the signing of a multilateral treaty to convert the Monroe Doctrine of the United States into an American Doctrine, in which would be proclaimed the inviolability of the principle of national autonomy, subordinate only to compulsory arbitration to settle differences among the countries on this side of the Atlantic, and the proscribing of all intervention.

The Montevideo Conference opened up new paths of mutual trust. The Mexican delegation not only planted the problem of non-intervention, but simultaneously, in line with the trend of national liberation upheld by Mexico and all the sister republics of America, the abolition of the Platt Amendment, which was a mistake of the United States, in the pursuit of a sincere Pan Americanism in accord with the desires of every one of the American nations.

The next year, Cuba and all of America were to see with deep satisfaction that the United States adhered to the ideal of true Pan Americanism by surrendering the right of intervention in Cuba granted by the Platt Amendment. The progress made in the Montevideo Conference was great and can be appreciated in the Convention on the Rights and Duties of States. This paved the way in the most reasonable fashion for filling in the gaps of the Monroe Doctrine, to transform it into what it really ought to be, a defense pact of all the countries of America against any overseas aggression, also a pact of security against hegemonies, against economic aggressions by any American countries against others of the continent.

Finally the Interamerican Conference of Consolidation and Peace at Buenos Aires was able to attain an ideal always sought and for so long proposed—an explicit, unanimous and unreserved condemnation of all intervention policy. All America subscribed to this Pact, which canceled a whole past of uneasiness and opened up a future of the sanest international comprehension, and which not only established immediate and concrete norms for the American nations but was also a stimulus and an example for the other countries of the world to achieve the grand universal ideal of peace.

The Buenos Aires conference gave to America and to the world the edifying principle embodied in Article I of the Additional Protocol Relative to Non-Intervention:

"The High Contracting Parties declare inadmissible the intervention of any one of them, directly or indirectly, and for whatever reason, in the internal or external affairs of any other of the Parties."

The Latin American ideal of collective and not unilateral continental defense was also achieved when the Convention for the "Maintenance, Preservation and Reestablishment of

Peace," and the "Declaration of Principles of Inter-American Solidarity and Cooperation," were signed. The latter proclaims in Article II:

"That every act susceptible of disturbing the peace of America affects each and every one of them, and justifies the initiation of the procedure of consultation provided for in the Convention for the Maintenance, Preservation and Reestablishment of Peace, executed at this Conference."

From that time on these principles have become firmly established and have gained fresh strength. They have been reinforced by positive acts that emphasize the sincerity and good faith with which they have been welcomed by all the peoples of the Americas.

After the United States renounced the Platt Amendment, in August of the same year (1934), in fulfillment of a promise made by President Roosevelt when passing through Haiti, the last United States forces still in that Republic were withdrawn. A new spirit of continental confidence and solidarity was evidenced by Declaration XV on "Reciprocal Assistance and Co-operation for the Defense of the Nations of the Americas," adopted at the Second Meeting of Ministers of Foreign Affairs of the American Republics, held at Havana, which provided:

"That any attempt on the part of a non-American State against the integrity or inviolability of the territory, the sovereignty or the political independence of an American State shall be considered as an act of aggression against the States which sign this declaration."

This attitude was emphasized by the spirit which characterized all the inter-American measures adopted at the Third Meeting of Consultation of the Ministers of Foreign Affairs of the American Republics, held at Rio de Janeiro just after Pearl Harbor.

On July 23, 1942, in Washington, Cordell Hull declared:

"The Government of the United States strove increasingly to promote peace on the solid foundation of law, justice, non-intervention, non-aggression and international collaboration, with growing insistence. We advocated the principles of a broad and constructive world order in political, economic, social, moral and intellectual relations among nations—principles which must constitute the foundation of any satisfactory future world order."

These are clear, austere words which I wish to set beside

those of another great American, the Foreign Minister of Uruguay, Dr. Alberto Guani, who, in his memorandum of June 21, 1941, referred to the maintenance of the safety and territorial integrity of our republics:

"The inclination of our peoples to strengthen the bonds that join the American body of nations was present from the beginning of their struggle for independence when the concept of country was broadened to include the sweep of the whole continent. American history in the past and present century offers many examples to show that this spirit still endures. Today it represents one of the strongest guarantees for the safety of the New World."

The doctrine of Latin America, and that to which the United States has given the name of its illustrious president, are like two rivers which have had their source in regions of storm and have flowed a long way in the same direction, each in its separate course, one straight, the other deflected by artificial causes, until they finally meet in one vast, overwhelming stream.

The shades of Bolívar and Monroe, now that the false interpreters of the latter have been thrown into the discard, may feel well satisfied today at the results of their work.

Hitler · VI

ON FEBRUARY 24, 1920, AT THE MUNICH Hofbrauhaus, a group held its first meeting. In the years to follow it was to become one of the most tragic moral perturbations ever recorded in the whole history of mankind.

About two thousand persons—mostly either false intellectuals or the dregs of the first great war of our century—gathered in that beer-hall amid the pleasant smoke of tobacco and the thicker, more stifling heat of nationalistic doctrines, to draw up a program that apparently aimed only at the political resurrection of Germany. The most important planks of this program were:

Union of all Germans to create a greater Germany.
Abolition of all German-Austrian peace treaties.
Acquisition of territories and colonies for surplus population.
Bestowal of German citizenship solely on persons of German blood.

Expulsion of Jews.

Abolition of all income not derived from actual labor. Confiscation of war profits.

Nationalization of commercial monopolies.

Agrarian reforms; if necessary, land confiscation.

Creation of a national army.

Control of the press for the promotion of German national interests.

Liberty of religious beliefs in such degree that they do not jeopardize the state.

Centralization of national authority.

Around the figure of a small, impetuous man named Adolf Hitler—who had failed as a painter and who had won a second-grade Iron Cross at the battle of Wytschaete—the German Workers' Party was formed. As the months passed, the name of the organization seemed rather meaningless to its author, for soon he added two more adjectives: national and socialist, joined by a queer hyphen, the ironical brevity of which sought to provide a bridge between two ideological worlds extremely difficult to couple together.

After a brief delay in 1923 caused by the failure of the Munich putsch, National Socialism made astoundingly rapid progress in German public opinion. From 2,000 members in 1920 and 17,000 in 1927, the party increased to 1,000,000 in 1928, to 6,400,000 in 1930, to 13,700,000 in 1932, to 17,265,823 in May, 1933, and to 39,655,288 in November of the same year.

What were the motives of the organization? Why did it arouse such remarkable response? And how was it able, in only thirteen years, to gain complete control of the political forces of Germany? The answers are of interest because they reveal the true character of national socialism: not creation but revenge; not constructive goals, but intolerance, rancor and destruction.

Since the age of Tiberius, liberty has had no enemies more persistent than those whom Dr. Marañon in his able psychological study of dictators calls "typical grudge-holders of history." If Nero had been a less grotesque poet, Marat a better physician, what disasters the tragic Rome of the Caesars and the benevolent Paris of '93 might have escaped!

It is significant that the National Socialist Party should have been the work of a resentful man, unable to adjust himself to the post-war order. Most significant also is the fact that his "program" tended to awaken all the dark passions hidden in those millions of discontented people who made up the energetic and industrious population of the Third Reich. This explains the extremely rapid advance of Hitler's doctrines, for actually no soil was better prepared for the sowing of violence than were the hearts of the German citizens, humiliated by the 1918 Armistice.

One must remember that a few years earlier this great country had reached the apex of military, economic and commercial power in Europe. The Allies, unable to destroy the sources of Prussian dynamism, merely wounded its pride without fully tearing down its elements of resistance, which in a short time were to give it a chance for dramatic revenge.

The 1914-18 war experience did not convince the German people of their weakness, but rather of the fundamental contradictions of the old order. Accordingly their thinkers did not try to understand the real causes of their defeat, but blamed all mankind, accusing it of decrepitude, as did Oswald Spengler in *The Decline of the West*. In short, if civilization had not served to guarantee the empire's success, it became convenient to distrust the great advantages of civilization. If Germany had failed to gain the hegemony of Europe, it was because Europe did not deserve the privilege of being ruled by so noble a master, the inevitable and final stage in her evolution.

The German leaders, quick to sense this murky pessimism, utilized it ably as a powerful leverage to arouse the angers smouldering in the whole community, which had reached the peak of technical progress without emerging from barbarian faith in force.

All this drives on to the immediate basic conclusion that thus far, however great the contributions of the German people to philosophy, music and science, its might has always constituted a menace for the spiritual values of mankind. This peril springs from the essential imperviousness of the Teutonic temperament to Christian civilization, which is based upon a free and Mediterranean concept of the Universe, something the professors of Ulm and Jena and Königsberg, though apparently they admired it with such enthusiasm, never loved.

To the idea of civilization, the German intelligentsia posed the contrary notion of culture—that Kultur, written with the initial "K" of Kaiser, Kolossal and Kommandantur—which so eloquently reveals their secret passion for mastery, for regimentation and mass production, and the subterranean militarization of minds and consciences.

Surely all genuine civilization implies freedom, whereas "culture" frequently converts itself into arrogance and the threat of thralldom. The cultured man is only an instrument, whereas the civilized man is a product. Civilization is an equilibrium to which culture brings only one important, but partial, element. For, to function properly, civilization requires the moral quotients of nobility, self-denial and tolerance.

Thus it was that Nazism found such an unusually fertile field in post-war Germany, for it flattered the non-human principle ever characteristic of German cultural processes: it opened to a resentful people a horizon of universal dimensions; and, in spite of its inarticulateness, it promised an organized world in which scientific progress would be imposed by force of arms, without regard for those scruples of spiritual freedom and independent judgment which the democracies always have defended.

Nations with the Mediterranean mentality (and all the great modern countries are such, including the United States and England because of their basic Christianity) consider that the State should not oppose the vital interests of the community. To Germans, the State is a supreme end in itself, to which individuals should adapt themselves. This faith in the power of juridical abstractions over the supposed experimental psychology of the collective spirit, is to be noted both in the philosophy of Hegel and the doctrines of Wundt. According to Hegel, law places the community's freedom above individual liberties; the State, according to his doctrines, is "the substance of the individual."

Thus is established the policy of absolutism, which, once the doctrine of force has been established, as Foullé points out, inevitably carries the state on to conquest and perpetual war. "The victorious nation is always stronger than the one subdued, and its very power is proof of its right! History, therefore, is the judgment of God, an everlasting God of Wrath!"

Totalitarianism—which in Russia obeyed an economic situation emanating from the dialectical concept of the class struggle, and which in Italy, Mussolini adopted as the means to achieve a resurrection of the Imperial City—in Germany has been a continuous military longing. From the garrisoned kingdom of Frederick I to the national socialism of Adolf Hitler, Germany has been carrying to the extreme the monstrous development of her attachment to the belief that the State is a material and moral entity distinct from the nation; that the State is something greater in right and authority, a greedy and voracious Moloch nourishing itself on the lives of its own devotees. Thus, while democracies consider that the State has no other purpose than the welfare and security of individuals, Prussian Germany sacrifices individuals on the altars of the greatness of the State.

These considerations suffice to explain why nationalism inevitably turned into a machine of oppression within and war without.

The pseudo-scientific bases of the system consisted first of a eulogy of race superiority and the Messianic predestination of Germany; and, second, of a Wagnerian exaltation of violence, with cruel contempt for the weak and the total annihilation of Christian philosophy, which Hitler, imitating Nietzche, would not hesitate to characterize as "the morality of slaves." The racial theses we shall consider in a subsequent chapter.

As for the Messianic predestination of Germany, the arrogance is so obvious that it does not even deserve detailed analysis. If we do not accept the dogma of superior race, how can we tolerate the assumption that there are chosen States, Prussia included, whose role can be to impose culture on other peoples by means of the lash or the howitzer?

The antinomy between Christianity and National Socialism is real, and is the most powerful argument that men of goodwill now thrust at totalitarian Germany. The Fuehrer acknowledged this when he told Hermann Rauschning in 1934 that, for his country, "religion is still a matter of major importance and that everything depends on knowing whether the Germans will continue to be faithful to the Jew-Christian worship and the servile morality of compassion, or whether they will adopt a new faith in the immanent god of the nation, i. e., a god inseparable from German fate and German blood."

In that religion, Goebbels would like to be the Mahomet, whereas Hitler already feels himself to be the mysterious and awful Wotan. His Valhalla is in Berchtesgaden, his Valkyries are Gestapo agents; legends of him circulate like the gold of the tetralogy, deep in the waters of father Rhine.

Equally remote from Luther and from the Vatican, the ideologists dream of inventing a Teutonic mythology, pitiless and unmerciful: a new order of heaven, in which moral goodness would be superseded by fear and in which the love of one's neighbor would be replaced by contempt for the weak. Starting from such premises, Hitler's program soon acquired its characteristic feature—permanent *coup d'etat*. This characteristic has to be sought for in the deeds perpetrated, not in the books of propaganda, which like *Mein Kampf* are hazy breviaries containing general ideas and autobiographical comments to promote public enthusiasm for their authors. Comparison of the thesis, largely Anglophile, of *Mein Kampf* with the evolution of Nazi policies at once reveals the deep gulf between the theory and the reality of dictatorships. Even so, some of the concepts in that book, written in the most verbose and abstract style, provide us with an almost involuntary confession. I quote them here:

"The pure-race German is the natural master of the American Continent, and always will be unless he sacrifices himself by incestuous contamination [with natives]."

"Whoever sincerely desires the triumph of peace, should do everything possible that the world be conquered by the Germans."

"In this world, success is the only judge."

"The rights of the German citizen should prevail over the rights of the foreigner. A street-sweeper in Berlin should consider himself more honored by being a citizen of the Reich than by being a king over another country."

"The first duty of propaganda is to win men for the purposes of the organization; the first duty of the organization is to win men for the continuation of the propaganda."

And this last fragment, apparently never read by Mussolini or the Emperor of Japan: "All that is truly great has never been won by a coalition, but by the triumph of a single victor."

Among other things, Nazism cites the following domestic aims:

Destruction of democracy.

Homogeneity in the population by eliminating Jews, sterilization of the sick and weak, suppression of alien minorities, and the annexation of German minorities imbedded, for the most part, in Austria, Poland and Czechoslovakia.

Economic autarchy.

Intensive militarization.

Crushing of the individual and the family, through a gradual poisoning of childhood by means of a deformed education, through a humiliating espionage which converts the brother into his own brother's informer, the son into an accuser of his own father, and the wife into a hypocritical betrayer of her husband.

Complete extirpation of the liberty of expression, conscience and thought. The burning of prohibited books and the exile of scholars; sale of modern museum paintings; censorship of all journals and the press.

Creation of a uniform crowd mind, determined by the State in universities and newspapers, thanks to the ceaseless efforts of the employees of the Ministry of Propaganda.

The complete suppression of legal guarantees won by the worker and the farmer; compulsory social labor.

All this program of subjugation does not even have as its purpose the stimulus of the ancient democracies that based their own liberty on the slavery of outsiders. As Ambassador George S. Messersmith expressed it recently in an address to the International Women's Club of Mexico City, the Nazi leaders "clearly affirm that first they will enslave their own nation and their people and then use them to enslave others."

The power obtained as a result of these various measures is utilized abroad for a policy of aggression, of threat and perpetual war. This policy needed a pretext, living space; and a technical excuse, the incapacity of the democracies. Supported by either one or both of these rhetorical arguments and always pretending that his ambitions were definitely limited in each concrete instance to the immediate sphere of the given victim, Hitler succeeded in reestablishing compulsory military service, thus violating the Versailles Treaty; in remilitarizing the Rhineland, thus violating the Locarno Pact; in annexing Austria in 1938; in invading Czechoslovakia in March, 1939; in annihilating Poland in September of the same year; in occupying Belgium, Denmark, the Netherlands, Norway and the Duchy of Luxembourg, and in overwhelming and splitting up France, in 1940; in crushing Yugoslavia and Greece in 1941; in invading Russia in 1941 and 1942. To serve his tragic schemes he dragged along his two contradictory allies: Italy, with a Mediterranean culture, antithetical to Germany in its temperament, its philosophy, and its Christian interpretation of life; and Japan, closely akin to Germany in ambition, in race arrogance, and in anti-Christian contempt for human pity.

The tactics for all these victories were always the same. Before all else, Germany deceived the enemy with promises she had no intention of fulfilling: the offering of a non-aggression pact; a guarantee of neutrality, while secretly planning a treacherous violation and, at the precise opportune moment, throwing the whole of her war machinery upon a single point after having underhandedly undermined the opponent's resistance by methodical fifth column infiltration consisting of espionage, bribery and propaganda.

Let us listen to Hitler's voice concerning this subject: "War is man's natural state. When I decide to declare war on France, it will be because I will have previously introduced into Paris in full peace time, troops wearing French uniforms, against whom no one will even think of wanting to fight. Stripped of their general staffs, countries fall into immediate chaos. But previously I shall have contacted men capable of constituting new governments that suit my requirements. We shall not even have to bribe such men. They will come of their own volition to solicit our protection because of their ambition, their own blindness and party discord."

On reading such words, one cannot tell whether a chief of state is speaking, or, as seems more likely, a cold sardonic gangster, teaching his accomplices the surest way to get hold of a bank, first by bribing the evil janitor, then if necessary, by chloroforming the loyal watchman.

When we reach this point we feel deeply what a terrible menace Nazi-Fascist expansion is for every country in the world. From the religious standpoint, National Socialist absolutism is opposed to all creeds, for it observes that each is the builder of a sanctuary of the conscience that cannot be breached by assault troops. In cultural matters, the totalitarian state finds itself in open opposition to freedom, which is the moral essence of all teaching. In the *Rheinische Westfälische Zeitung*, October 15, 1934, we take note of these words, addressed to a student audience by Herr Franck, one of the "official" thinkers of the Nazi regime:

"What you ought to look for is not the joy of saying, 'I have discovered a wholly new idea, a theory entirely apart from what my fellow students have thus far believed.' No! The decisive question should be: 'Will my scientific discovery aid the cause of National Socialism?'"

Nowadays German universities do not reveal truth, merely the official "truth" of the regime. Degrees are not awarded to the most diligent students, but to those who most assiduously attend Party meetings; to those who utter the most aggressive ideas, and to those who have made the largest number of secret accusations against friends and the members of their own families.

A sentence revealing this tyrannical dogmatism is found in one of Doctor Goebels' speeches: "Like the good Nazis we are, we are convinced that we are right. For this reason we do not permit others to tell us they are right, too, for if they actually are right, then they are National Socialists, and if they are not National Socialists, then how can they be right?"

For the same reason that education has been prostituted to the level of debased propaganda, justice has come to be a barren word, scarcely serving to conceal the exactions of authority, scarcely able to provide a legal mask for the most shameful frauds. Where force prevails, what does law mean? The judge must obey the policeman, and the law becomes, at best, a police regulation.

As for economic life, the Nazi-Fascist abuses are quite as

vexatious as in judicial, educational and religious fields. Lacking currency acceptable in world markets, Hitler's government has invented a legal mark whose domestic value is several times greater than that quoted for it by the most liberal foreign money-exchange. This money is not backed by actual financial deposits but is guaranteed by the military force utilized to impose it. Rifle in hand, the Nazi soldier—agent of the government that issues the false money—causes it to circulate through all vassal territories, and with it obtains merchandise, which the subject people must buy at gold prices or with currency issued by an honestly administered bank.

If this goes on within the country, what shall we say of what occurs abroad? Hostages are shot; priests die of hunger in concentration camps; populations, compelled to give up their harvests and their products for paper money, must accept a rationing in tiny doles that is but an insignificant part of that which their masters confiscated; war prisoners, wholly cut off from their families for years, are used as hostages to encourage, at a three-to-one rate, an emigration of workers that will leave the occupied regions in ever more drastic conditions of misery and decay.

Legitimate institutions, which in Germany are mere whims of the dictator, have disappeared from the cities conquered by Hitler's armies. The Brussels burgomaster is in jail. The same has happened to almost every true municipal authority in Belgium, Holland and Luxembourg. In Berlin the Reichstag meets now and then, not to express political opinion, but to applaud the Caesar and obey his commands.

While accusing the democracies of corruption, the German leaders have piled up huge fortunes; while criticizing the lack of culture among free peoples, Hitler's ministers have stripped the museums of the defeated countries and have carried the sculptures and paintings off to their own homes. Albert Einstein and Thomas Mann live in exile. Stephan Zweig and his wife committed suicide; hundreds of teachers, scholars and poets eat the bitter bread of ostracism.

An immense nation, with limitless technical potentialities, finds itself under the orders of these ferocious and delirious masters. And this is the nation that a century ago awakened the awe and admiration of men with the *Seventh Symphony*, the Second *Faust*, the *Critique of Pure Reason*, and so many masterpieces of poetry, music and thought.

We already have seen by what chain of circumstances the heirs of Goethe, of Kant, of Handel and of Beethoven are now fighting to reduce the whole world to shameful submission.

When reason once more rules, the docile slaves of Hitler's caprices will remember this epoch as a ruinous madness. Everything is a perishing triumph of cruelty: its concept of force, its defense of crime and its hatred for liberty.

In the face of totalitarian madness, the Americas, together with the democracies of Europe and Asia, rise up determined never to compromise and to struggle without flinching to restore the world to a condition in which man shall not lose the dignity of being a man.

E *Imperialism* · VII

EVERY PRACTICAL-MINDED AMERICAN CAPABLE of sensing the grandeur of the proposed union of the American peoples, cannot but wonder whether the proper materials are available with which to raise the structure of this ideal.

Can we rely on the generous policy announced; on the declarations made by Roosevelt, Hull, Wallace and Welles? We must consider whether this policy is only the determination of a party or of nobly inspired men, or something more than that, a new direction being taken by international conscience, and whether it is based on community of interests and ideals, the only firm foundation for any permanent policy.

Are the eloquent words of Doctor Eduardo Santos in his Presidential message to the Colombian Congress on July 20, 1939, true? "The most encouraging note at this dark hour of the world has been struck by the policy of the United States; it must daily ring louder for it is definitely aimed at securing the right to peace. Every reason, both idealistic and of expedience, supports and defends this policy. What on other continents might seem contrary to national needs and aspirations, on our continent harmonizes perfectly with them."

Up to now, the solidarity of our Latin American peoples has not got beyond the stage of emotional brotherhood. As for the United States, the Good Neighbor Policy represents an international system upheld by the group now in power, in a nation where political parties from time to time alternate as proof of genuine democracy. Consequently the best prospects that a given international policy will endure must be sought in permanent causes, both material and spiritual. These causes, no doubt, do exist. They will be reviewed and will lead us to the conclusion that continental unity is going to go forward, either with the will of the statesmen who now rule the destinies of our various nations, or without it, for such union is the expression of a new technical civilization and of a strong international awareness, day by day operating more decisively to shape the course of human destiny.

Rapid communications, improved transportation and means for the diffusion of ideas have brought about unity of intent and purpose. When physical distances between men's minds have been abolished, what do barriers between nations mean? Neither more nor less than thin blue lines on maps. Even ocean-girt continents can hardly feel that they are separate units. Of course, in the Old World, despite the closeness of the peoples, there are unsurmountable frontiers of hate, enmity and prejudice. But America is still free from such deplorable legacies. True enough, closer contact between peoples may serve either to facilitate the subjection of the weaker or to set up cooperation between them. Unity, then, will arise from methods either based on force or emanating from the free will of the peoples. Which path have the Americas chosen?

What stands out at first glance, and on this we most strenuously insist, is that the basic causes that hindered the free flow of confidence among all the nations of the continent have swiftly and definitely been disappearing.

Among those causes, none is so redoubtable as the marked and definite decline in the United States of Big Business—the trusts and monopolies—as an all-powerful force controlling international and domestic policies. Increasingly the trusts and monopolies are being replaced by the overmastering power of the genuine American people.

A fake plutocratic democracy (that "plutodemocracy" of which Goebbels spoke) has been overthrown during the last two decades. Its place is being occupied by a true government of the people, by the people, for the people.

The consequence of economic policies motivated exclusively by the profit-motive, like blind forces flowing from the industrial revolution, has been minutely analyzed by advanced writers. Those consequences belong to the last stage of human oppression and man's fight to achieve social justice.

Up to now we have been studying the various forms of servitude due to misery and man's inability to master the forces of nature without the necessary equipment and material means. However, there is another form of servitude within the realm of applied science, in the development of the machine, in mass technological production. This form of servitude forms part of the picture in highly industrialized countries. There the growing concentration of wealth in the hands of a few privileged individuals or corporations has subjected great masses of workers to the cruel hardships of uncertainty, unemployment and iniquitous exploitation.

The days of anguish and despair through which the masses have lived since the advent of the industrial revolution constitute one of the most somber aspects of human suffering. Apostles and philosophers, visionaries and men of action, have inch by inch been achieving social justice for the working classes.

In America, it is the United States, despite the unusually favorable conditions surrounding its material growth, that has borne the heavy burden of a highly industrial and technical civilization, not yet founded on standards of economic justice. The inequality in the distribution of wealth in the United States is startlingly defined in figures presented by Charles A. Beard and George H. E. Smith in their book, *The Old Deal and the New:*

"From an analysis of individual net income statistics, it appears that 38,892 individuals got dividends of $2,562,000,000 in 1929. These individuals did not number more than one per cent of all stockholders, yet they received forty-four per cent of all dividends paid. Their dividend receipts (comprising only part of the income these people received) were equal to more than one-fifth of the wages paid to 8,800,000 wage-earners in manufacturing; or to one-half the wages paid to 4,500,000 persons employed in retail trade; or approximately one-fourth of the cash value of 6,300,000 farmers' products in 1929."

Cycles of prosperity and depression have exposed large sections of the American people to the gloomy consequences of unemployment. A system of agonizing economic insecurity has extensively underlaid the outward surface of material and constructive splendor of that great manufacturing nation.

It is not only the laboring classes that, over a painful march of more than a century, have felt the insecurity of the capitalistic system, under such characteristic forms as low salaries, unemployment, and inhuman working conditions. The middle classes, whose patiently accumulated savings have so often been swallowed up by the whirlpool of unscrupulous speculation, or small farmers whose holdings have been foreclosed by unpaid creditors or bank failures, have also had the evils of the system painfully brought home to them. Even in the realm of plutocracy itself, the tycoons now and then have gone to their doom and collapsed in obedience to the fiat of Wall Street. Insecurity from base to apex—this has been the heritage of several successive generations, in a nation that has achieved the most remarkable progress chronicled in history, but has never been able to do away with distress unfairly inflicted on the large majority of the population.

Imperialism and wild speculation also arose, begotten of that same blind capitalist scheme of things. These two forces that gnawed at the very heart of true democracy—social injustice within the United States, imperialism that destroyed the prosperity and confidence of the American peoples—show, by their common origin and simultaneous disappearance, that they are the bitter fruits of an evil system and not a product of the national consciousness of the United States.

Imperialism has been defined in many different ways, and over the years and the continents has pursued diverse methods and routes. Modern imperialism finds its concrete description in the Renaissance when Machiavelli formulated the theory of the inevitability of territorial expansion. The development of commerce and the discovery of America followed earlier precedents in their mode of colonization. Colonies are founded by emigrants from the mother country who go out to exploit the land, the mines, the forests. This form of imperialism has been the natural outgrowth of the European system which has sought empty spaces for its excess population. In Latin America it also had a religious motivation, the effort to incorporate the natives into the Christian faith. The colony, with all its injustices, with all its faults, springs from the womb of the mother country; the aborigines are destroyed, as in the United States, or assimilated, as in Mexico. Where the native population was not destroyed, the mixing of the colonizer with the native has been invigorating and fruitful. But for all the splendor of this form of imperialism by territorial expansion, it passes through grave periods of crisis. In the country most practicing this type of imperialism, the Utilitarian and the Manchester schools repudiated territorial expansion. And Gladstone himself even opposed recognition of the policy of commercial expansion.

Later there arose a new form of imperialism in the world, one more hateful, for it evades the responsibility that was assumed by colonizing imperialism. The latter opened up new territories to economic development under a stimulation that was in any case a civilizing force and that also enriched the mother country. In contrast, commercial imperialism is characterized by a small caste of military rulers, who subject alien populations to forced labor, or by an inhuman caste of trusts or monopolies, who organize the economic exploitations of a country. In the first instance, the colony, for all its injustices, generates its own independence. In the second, the subjugated peoples have no other hope than to take advantage of the set-backs of the "empires" and the struggles among them.

Imperialism has a long history, but this book proposes merely to refer to the imperialism of the last few decades.

Mechanization, the transformation of the small shop into the big factory, the growing output of manufacturers of every kind and the enormous expansion and increased speed of the means of transport, made it imperative to acquire raw materials and assured markets, even though whole peoples had to be thrown into bondage.

Cotton brought about the occupation of Egypt and Burma; rubber was the lure in the Congo, the Malay Peninsula and the Dutch East Indies; copra led to the conquest of the South Sea Islands; and petroleum explains the dismemberment of the Ottoman Empire, many of the warlike vicissitudes of these last few years and the major chapters of the financial imperialism of the United States.

Before the present war, more than half the surface of the earth and over a thousand million human beings dwelt under the thralldom or "protection" of ten imperialistic States. For each man, woman and child in the British Isles, there were ten men working in the colonies. France's colonial empire covered an area twenty times greater than that of the republic. Little Portugal's foreign possessions are twenty-three times as big as that peninsular nation, while Holland and Belgium are like tiny tugs towing gigantic transports.

In Gladstone's time, anti-imperialistic feeling in England came to a head. It was induced by the collapse of other mighty colonial empires, which showed how costly colonies were, how inevitable the loss of the effort exerted to build them up. But in 1870 Great Britain produced half the world's steel; her foreign commerce was double that of her closest rival, and steam-driven factories turned out all kinds of goods with a speed and perfection equaled by none. Besides possessing the most powerful navy in the world, she had to be sure of markets and sources of raw materials wherever available.

In 1875 only ten per cent of Africa had been appropriated by the European nations; a few years later, all of it had been divided up. The reason was that in the last quarter of the nineteenth century, Germany, France and the United States became industrialized in competition with Great Britain and clamored for their "places in the sun." At the turn of the century the United States led the world in steel production, and Germany began to forge ahead of England.

The rising imperialism of these nations compelled England, which a few years before had shown symptoms of wanting to abandon her imperialistic policy, to claim the lion's share of every transaction and spoliation, just to maintain her prestige. Apart from this, the essential raw materials needed by Europe were mainly commodities originating in tropical regions unhealthy for white men and therefore not suitable for colonization. This was why Nigerian and Congolese Negroes, Malays, Hindus, and even denizens of the Western Hemisphere, before the Monroe Doctrine was strong enough to prevent it, had to be reduced to subjection. They were needed to extract rubber, fibers, oil, hardwoods and exotic fruits.

Obeying these causes, the imperialist mechanism works very simply: the primitive trading post complains of the violation of special privileges or treaties, and troops are sent to occupy the surrounding territory and reduce the natives to subjection. In other cases, explorers or missionaries appeal for help, and an army takes possession of the country. Another method is to make loans or investments in the hope that they will not be repaid, so as to collect them swollen by usurious interest. Thus seizure of the soil is consummated and the dwellers on it are disposed of as goods and chattels. Another and easier way is to divide up other people's land, including the enslaved inhabitants, under some sort of a political compromise.

As typical cases of transfers to governments of the commercial interests of private companies, we may cite the following:

In 1798 the government of Holland took over the Dutch East India Company. Not content to go on collecting from petty kings and native chiefs the usual tax "in kind," the Netherlands government, under the pretext, among others, of lessened returns from certain crops, formerly highly esteemed, forced the natives to grow sugar, coffee, tobacco, tea, cacao, etc. The method pursued by Governor Daendels faithfully illustrates this imperialistic stage. He ordered every family in the coffee growing sections to plant and tend at least a thousand trees. Two-fifths of the crop went to the State as a tax; the other three-fifths had to be sold to the State, at a price it fixed. In this way profitable crops were promoted.

In 1858 Great Britain took over the interests of the private companies that had been trading with India and thereby began the conquest of the vast peninsula, affording a perfect picture of imperialistic domination. In 1900 the British Government compensated a company that enjoyed a monopoly of commerce with Nigeria, and without further formality declared a protectorate over both northern and southern Nigeria. On the other hand, Algeria and Morocco were conquered by France under the pretext of intervening in behalf of her nationals, a plea very generally utilized to justify imperialistic adventures, as in the past in many countries of the Americas.

The same argument was turned to account by Italy to precipitate the war with Turkey, which gave her Tripoli and Cyrenaica. Like pretexts, interwoven with the expansion of old trading posts, led to the "protection" of Tongking and Cambodia in 1863. Later, in 1883, a war with China was provoked that by 1887 had consolidated, for France's benefit, her grip on the rich prize of French Indo-China.

A careful study of these instances will illustrate the dangers inherent in the mechanism of direct conquest. The danger lies not so much in the resistance of the peoples wronged as in the jealousy of rival powers. In the Congo episode in 1881, De Braza, by stealing a march on Stanley, then employed by the King of the Belgians, took possession of the country lying north of the Lower Congo River, and set two rival imperialisms face to face with each other. After that came the Fashoda incident, in 1898, between Colonel Marchand and Lord Kitchener. The result of this was to check unilateral conquest and bring about the partition of Africa by common accord with every European Power motivated by greed. They intrigued and compromised diplomatically to avert armed conflict.

This is also well illustrated by the Congress of Berlin in 1878, when Turkey ceded Cyprus to England to prevent Russia from seizing the island. As compensation, Russia in turn was to share with England influence in the Balkans and Armenia, while France was given Tunis as her slice. In 1884 Great Britain recognized Portugal's sovereignty over the Lower Congo, to put a spoke in the wheel of the King of the Belgians; but, forced to yield ground when both France and Germany frowned on the arrangement, then had to consent to Germany's taking the Belgian Congo within her sphere of influence, an affront which Belgium wiped out when in 1918 she obtained a mandate over a portion of Germany's former colonies.

In like manner, the division of the Ottoman Empire was

planned about the middle of the last century. The Crimean War was a Franco-British move to halt Russia's ambitions. At the Berlin Congress, the fate of Bosnia, Herzegovina, and other Balkan countries, at that time vassals of Turkey, was settled. In 1891 the Anglo-Italian Treaty was signed, practically leaving Abyssinia in Italy's hands. After Fashoda, England and France "amicably" divided up the Sudan.

A review of the secret treaties, pacts, settlements and other somber combinations by which the partition of the world was consummated would be interminable.

The Algeciras Conference marks the peak of diplomatic control over imperialism by equilibrating antagonistic ambitions. In connection with the Morocco issue, the right to independence of that nation was recognized, subject to apportionment of its territory into French and Spanish zones of influence. Tangiers was internationalized and substantial concessions were made in favor of Germany, including economic exploitation of the territory on an equal footing. All this, of course, was decided upon without consulting the Moroccans.

Is it strange, therefore, that the roars and growls of the wild beasts tearing at their helpless victims have never ceased to disturb world peace? Is it to be wondered that this law of the jungle should continue to lead to the most frightful catastrophes mankind has ever experienced?

Economic compromises also have been a pet proceeding of imperialists, not only for the purchase of uninhabited regions, or in agreement with the interests of the inhabitants, but covering other people's property and effected without other warrant than brute force. So, in 1890, Germany was awarded Heligoland in exchange for "her share" of Uganda, Zanzibar and Nyassaland. The completion of the Suez Canal in 1869 sealed the fate of Egypt. The big loans made to win dual control by France and England up to 1883 brought England in to protect the waterway. Thirty million pounds sterling invested in cotton plantations and advances to satisfy the whims of the Khedive led to England's taking possession of Egypt and looking upon the land as her property.

That was how, by straight conquest, diplomatic intrigues or commercial give and take, the greater part of the nations of the earth have been the playthings of the ambitions and rivalry of the Great Powers. In this stage banking and industry are the central forces of imperialism. Commerce, railways, military forces and bureaucracy are auxiliary factors. Industry needs cheap raw materials and good markets for its products, and applies to the banks for funds to keep up its output. Growing credits stimulate trade, that seeks sources of raw materials and outlets for its manufactured goods. Investments are made abroad to assure a supply of such cheap raw materials and the control of markets. Backward countries are taken unawares by payment of low prices for their natural wealth—whose value they fail to realize—and resale to them of manufactured goods, which they are themselves unable to produce, at exorbitant prices. After that, if the enslaved people ask for raises in wages and begin to commit the mortal sin of manufacturing goods for their own needs, industry, banking and commerce appeal to their government to chastise the subject nation.

Railway and steamship lines, whose profits increase with colonial traffic; militarists, who enjoy an easy means to distinction by winning lands; and the bureaucracy, for whose members posts and juicy sinecures are created, are all cogs in the gearing of this imperialistic machinery.

One feels, as one looks at these sad realities, that the world lives in a devilish ferment of rivalry, hatred, greed, rapine and gross injustice, that can lead only to war. No dream of peace can come true in this rank jungle of predatory instincts. This explains why one of the most insistent cries that goes up from the United Democracies is that imperialism be scrapped once and for all.

Even before the present war certain apparently disconnected events were pregnant with a clear hint that this stage of western imperialism was approaching its end.

The first World War represents the failure of diplomatic procedure to keep imperialism within bounds. It is well-known that the unfair distribution of African colonies, the occupation of Morocco by France, contrary to the Algeciras covenant; the controversy between England and Germany over the Constantinople-Baghdad Railway and the position of the Balkan nations inside the swiftly crumbling Turkish Empire were the main causes of that gigantic world conflagration. However, for a time it seemed to have been averted because a secret treaty had been concluded between England and Germany, dividing up Portugal's colony of Mozambique. But other pacts provided for the delivery of Mesopotamia and Smyrna to England, Syria and Northern Anatolia to France, and Northern Mesopotamia, Southern Anatolia and Northern Syria, to Germany.

Besides all this, the railway from Constantinople to Baghdad was to be built by English, British, French and German financial interests. Only Russia was dissatisfied, unless given Constantinople and the control over the Dardanelles. However, in March, 1914, Germany proposed that she and Russia exercise common control over this water gateway. The only obstacle, that finally did let loose the dogs of war, was Austria's Balkan policy, which Germany refused to disavow.

That frightful slaughter should, for the reasons stated, have been a splendid lesson in anti-imperialism. Unfortunately, this was not so.

The war that broke out in 1914, essentially a clash between rival imperialisms, resolutely attempted to prolong the system of dividing up the booty. In fact, while the contest was still on, France, Britain and Russia concluded agreements for the distribution of the German colonies and the Turkish Empire. Furthermore, under the secret Treaty of London, concluded in April, 1915, Italy's entrance into the war was purchased by a promise to turn over to her substantial slices of the Turkish dominions. However, when peace was concluded, an unexpected factor came in that upset all these plans. This was President Wilson's idealism, which advocated the readjustment of the colonial problem raised by subjection of the peoples victimized by imperialism, through the adoption of the principle of self-determination.

A strict application of Wilson's ideal would have meant the complete destruction of all "imperialistic" ambitions, through the liberation of subject peoples. As was to be expected, Mr. Wilson's proposal could not prevail, but was strong enough to bring about a compromise, in the form of "mandates" under the League of Nations. But it did not protect Germany's colonies, or the Turkish Empire, which became the classic spoils of imperialistic victory. Nevertheless it was applied to a number of countries and peoples that were turned over to the Great Powers under "mandates," with the understanding that in the near future they would become capable of self-government. It need hardly be observed that the Great Powers, as a mere formality, assented to the infant creation and solemnly gave their approval to the League mandates. In practice, however, they continued to dispose of them in every way as their own property, in imperialistic fashion. That being so, period after period expired and neither were mandates performed nor autonomous governments set up.

And yet there have been, after all, tentative attempts at self-determination. The case of Nigeria is impressive and conclusive proof against the system of subjection and forced labor. England made the experiment of leaving the Negroes of the Niger country and the Gold Coast free to cultivate their land and dispose of their crops at their own will. The old system of concessions operating on the basis of starvation wages and compulsory labor was abolished. All England kept was the monopoly of foreign trade, which she exercised very intelligently. The result was the enrichment of the natives, accompanied by an enormous increase in their productive capacity and purchasing power. This is shown by the fact that the imports of the Gold Coast were in 1920 ten times greater per capita than those of the Belgian Congo and French West Africa, contiguous and probably richer territories. In this way, with comparative liberty for the Negroes and their happy and satisfied co-operation, the British Government and British trade rapidly increased their revenues and earnings.

Similarly, India, into which the English first went to trade and which was later conquered to extract her products and raw materials, was on the brink of industrialization when the First World War broke out. This process would have resulted in almost entire liberty, in exchange for a British monopoly to govern her finances, which would in turn have imposed certain conditions on her foreign trade. If war had not broken out, and if Hindu nationalism had not blocked development of the plan, India would in a short time have become the most finished example of the full evolution of imperialism, from its most rudimentary to its most modern form.

Lastly, the sleeping giant that sprawls north and south of the mighty Yangtze Kiang was destined to exemplify, had not the war broken out, new stages of economic slavery. The European Powers, after battering down with cannon China's gateways and establishing trading "concessions," attempted to grab portions of her territory. The war between Japan and China, in 1894, was a clear case of armed conquest. In 1898, "leases" of seaports and maneuvers to obtain mining and railway grants and franchises marked the tendency to seize Chinese soil. Port Arthur, Kiau-Chau and Wei-Hai-Wei are notorious examples of that trend. Russia, Japan, England and Germany began to penetrate China to obtain control over large areas of the Flowery Kingdom. The 1914 War eliminated Germany, but by 1916 a complete partition of China by France, England, Russia and Japan had been planned. A somewhat indefinite interest was to be allowed the United States. However, China's nationalist revolution made the Europeans realize what a tough job it would be to conquer regions so remote, with an enormous population whose principal weapon consisted in passive and prolonged resistance. This was why, in 1920, an imperialistic consortium was formed among England, France, Japan and the United States. In it two opposing tendencies arose: the Japanese, which advocated a system of spheres of influence over certain regions as preliminary to military occupation and complete subjection; and the American, which recommended the Open Door and freedom of opportunity so that all four Powers might participate financially in the development of China's resources. The conquest of Manchukuo and Japan's undeclared war against China, a prelude to the present World War, brought this conflict of views to a head.

The war broke out when the new form of imperialism, financial imperialism, was well under way.

This kind of imperialism has one distinguishing feature; it involves a policy of capitalist-finance conquest. It is no longer individual, no conqueror carries it out; it is no longer a commercial enterprise; it is the imperialism of the nations, or better said, of the governments.

The enormous factories of the present day require a mighty stream of raw materials, at low prices, for upon this depend good wages for workers and reasonable cost of production for the finished goods, which must face competition in world markets. On the other hand, parts of the world, rich in raw materials, are inhabited by men with little money, and are industrially undeveloped. In them are united the two conditions big business requires to prosper. And so the stronger industrial nations, by means of extensive and intricate economic and financial consortiums—cartels, trusts, industrial syndicates —catch these countries in a network of investments and credits. They exploit the raw materials at their own prices, obstruct the establishment of competing factories, and what they give with one hand, in the form of starvation wages, they take away with the other by collecting payment for their industrial products at arbitrary prices also fixed by them. Their aim is to gain inordinate profits by keeping prices at unfairly high levels. Monopolists have never hesitated to boost the price of a given article. The means used have ranged from tariff barriers to actual blockades, from arbitrary distribution of production to a partial destruction of it, even in the case of food products urgently needed to relieve hunger in other countries.

The same or similar methods are often employed against other nations looked upon as rivals, or those which it is deemed desirable to keep in a precarious position. Countries thus colonized are truly and positively the slaves of their economic masters. Barely to subsist at the lowest living standards, they have to extract from the bowels of the earth, copper, zinc, lead, tin and petroleum; strip their forests of valuable hardwoods; labor to produce cotton, rubber, fibers, coffee, bananas, sugar or vegetable oils. In exchange for that enormous wealth thus drawn off and in many cases consumed beyond all possibility of replacement, and side by side with fabulous personal fortunes obtained by a few natives, we have expensive imported goods and a tottering national economy, lacking any firm basis, in the countries thus despoiled; a plentiful crop of hatred and ill-will, which, despite the weakness of the countries subjected to this colonizing process, is liable to become a source of grave danger at critical moments in history.

Thus two exceedingly valuable elements are lost to civilization: the cultural development of the exploited peoples, and the rise of a flourishing and steadily increasing body of consumers.

It would take too long to review the injustice, cruelty and abuse involved by this method of winning markets and raw materials. But one of the worst angles of this vicious organization of world economy should be pointed out: the competition that arises in nations economically powerful, interested in monopolizing this kind of conquest. This is the laboratory wherein war is compounded. Peace, thus menaced, is nothing less than an accumulation of high explosives, on the top of which our civilization sits ever more insecurely.

In its American aspect, economic imperialism has often led to abominably undemocratic influences. The rulers of some of the countries thus brought under subjection become the tools of big alien monopolies, in exchange for support in power against the will of the peoples whose rights were infringed and who are precluded from all opportunity of directing the national destinies into the channels of democratic institutions. This sets up a terrible equation: local tyranny within and economic oppression from without.

The two last wars, but especially the one we are now passing through, have shown the fallacy of calculations made by imperialism in attempts to gain markets and raw materials by war. In reality neither are markets ensured nor raw materials gained.

Abuses by the strong in times of peace are easily sustained, especially in the case of weak nations; but when wars break out, such abuses fail to ensure the support of the latter, and at such times no enemy is small enough to be despised.

It has already been demonstrated that in our time conquest is a negative method. Raw materials are important, but so are the men that live on the land and produce them. Conquest temporarily ensures a supply of the inert material, but the men are lost. In contrast, co-operation places other people's land at the service of every nation peacefully. It assures a supply of raw materials and wins friendship.

For a long time past, imperialism has become inconvenient.

First, because it is poor business. Then, because it is an international danger, both in peace and in war. Lastly, because the world conscience rejects it.

As happened in the times of Dom Pedro of Brazil in the case of slavery, the statesmen of our day will soon feel ashamed of having to bolster up an ignominious system. Jefferson said that he trembled for his country when he thought how just God was. Other statesmen who are parties to iniquitous subjugation of peoples also shudder when they think of it.

The fact is admitted that many of the reverses sustained by imperialistic nations are a consequence of past errors. But after the war, all the accumulated experiences will serve to cleanse and to create the new standards to be set up. Then will strike the hour of the confederation of peoples with the inherent right to create a noble destiny; then will strike the hour of the co-operation of the free peoples, above all, for those countries which will have a decisive influence in the organization of the world on the arrival of victory. England, despite her mistakes, is unquestionably the nation that has established in the world the new forms of free government, and she is the inspired teacher of those constitutional systems that have succeeded in crystallizing peace based on human liberty and dignity. The trend is toward the light, toward Christian civilization. As regards the United States, and indeed the whole of America, those constitutional methods are a mighty and decisive propelling force to sweep away all the old forms of exploiting humanity, by substituting deep faith in co-operation between men and peoples.

Lastly, the three great inseparably knit forces that promote the ideal of the unity of the peoples and co-operation among them, instead of violence and subjection, are the progress of modern technology, democracy and the rise of the new international conscience. These forces will render useless the bloodstained paths of imperialism.

The proof of these vigorous tendencies will be found in the declarations from time to time made by the great spiritual guides of the present conflict.

Clement Attlee, British labor leader, on November 19, 1939, said that it is indispensable that imperialism be renounced and that the principle be accepted, in governing the colonies or territories to which an independent administration can not yet be granted, that the interests of the natives come first; that all nations ought to have equal access to markets and raw materials. This, he averred, can be achieved by an ample and reinforced system of mandates, under an international authority. His view is that a redistribution of colonial territories among rival imperialisms does not constitute a solution, for he does not admit the right of any nation to hold others in subjection.

Mr. Attlee's opinion coincides with declarations recently made by Secretary of State Hull, who, speaking of the right of nations to liberty and independence, declared that not all the peoples of the world are ready for liberty or able to defend it when the morrow comes, but all want a goal set toward which they can work, some guarantee that a date has been fixed for the realization of their ideals.

The declarations made by the governments of Great Britain and the United States of their intention to waive the rights of extraterritoriality privileges enjoyed by them in China, are of course highly eloquent, and their recent fulfillment still more effective.

Sumner Welles, in a speech delivered in the Arlington National Cemetery May 30, 1942, said movingly that "the era of imperialism has come to an end." It is necessary, he declared, to recognize the right of all peoples to be free, in the same way that the civilized world for a long time recognized the right of each individual to enjoy personal liberty. The principles of the Atlantic Charter must be implanted and made secure in the whole world, without excepting any ocean or continent whatsoever.

Vice-President Wallace, in his speech at Los Angeles on September 16, 1942, on the occasion of the celebration of the anniversary of Mexico's independence, categorically stated that all forms of imperialism, whether economic, political or cultural, were dead and buried.

Lastly, and as proof that these sentiments are shared by the whole American people, we have just read the declaration by Mr. Wendell Willkie after his visit to the Eastern fronts: "As Americans," asserted the man who opposed Mr. Roosevelt at the last election, "we must also realize that we share . . . the responsibility of making the whole world a commonwealth of free nations."

T The Americas and Democracy · VIII

THEIR VOCATION FOR DEMOCRACY, TOGETHER with their geographic position, forms a bond among the peoples of the Americas that is their common denominator. Some historians claim that the peoples of pre-Columbian days were dimly prescient of democratic forms of government. Unquestionably the different races inhabiting the Western Hemisphere were all preponderant, if not always conscious, factors in the emancipation movements initiated with the American Revolution. These movements broke out with surprising simultaneity —considering the scanty means of communication available at the beginning of the nineteenth century—and the similarity of their aims is an almost miraculous forecast of the solidarity now existing among the twenty-one republics of our hemisphere.

Whatever the explanation, it is amazing that the colonies now an integral part of the American Union, and those formerly belonging to Spain, should have chosen a form of government which theoretically is the most democratic of all.

For centuries they had been dependencies of monarchical states and yet they became republics, and from that time until now they have been consistently loyal to the institutions adopted when they embarked on an independent existence.

It is true that an empire was proclaimed in Mexico, but its brief duration is unimpeachable proof that it failed to satisfy genuine popular aspirations. Nor is our thesis contradicted by Maximilian's empire, an exotic importation bolstered up by foreign bayonets, which the people of the one-time Aztec capital greeted with the amusing cry of "Long live the Emperor of the Mexican Republic!" Neither do the tragic experiments in what is now the Haitian Republic destroy our contention.

If the Empire endured many years in Brazil, this was not so much due to any roots the system had among the people of that country, but to its unquestionable liberalism. The democratic spirit of Brazil's laws and inhabitants was much more genuine than that in some American lands organized as republics.

Not in all instances have popular institutions developed in strict accord with democratic procedure. We have had to endure dictatorships, now blood-stained, now paternal, that have been a denial of democratic aspirations. Despite this, the fact that even the most overbearing satraps have never dared destroy completely the republican theory of government is enlightening. There was a lingering trace of decency, an almost superstitious feeling that it would be a sacrilege to deprive the people of every hope of better times and of freedom.

Among the American nations following the path of democracy undoubtedly the most perfect example is the American Union.

The highest contribution made by the United States to the difficult science of free government is its written constitution, wrought by the people itself.

For the preservation of public liberties, an elastic yet reliable machinery was essential, to keep proper balance between two encroaching powers: the authorities and the multitude.

The American constitution, by a marvelous mechanism of "checks and balances," succeeded in establishing the bases for such equilibrium: the division of powers, the sovereignty of the states, the limitation of authority, and the supremacy of the courts. It established a system of government that has weathered every storm and has been consecrated by the greatness of the nation that has applied it firmly and loyally.

When Hamilton, in 1787, addressed the people to explain the transcendent importance of the new Magna Charta, he asserted that by their conduct and example, the people of the United States would determine whether human societies were capable of organizing a good government, the fruit of reflection and free choice by the citizenry, or whether they would be condemned to dwell always subjected to the contingencies of force in their political organization.

Throughout human history, humanity had sought constantly to attain liberty. But its most noteworthy efforts always had been ill-directed and amateurish, invariably ending in futile and painful movements, like that promoted by Spartacus.

To give permanence to a movement for freedom, a standard, a constitution, was necessary. To raise it to the rank of a boon available to the whole of humanity, universality of principles was necessary, and both these things are to be found in the Constitution of the United States, adopted in 1789.

The prosperity of the United States, under the liberties enjoyed, soon became a living example to other peoples attempting to overthrow the tyrannies that kept them in subjection. The French Revolution and the independence movements of the more southerly American States drew strength and inspiration from the independence and the institutions of the northern republic.

The 1789 constitution was framed by men eminent not only for their patriotism, but also for their previous accomplishments. Philosophers, jurists, graduates of English universities who had practised at the colonial bar, men skilled in the art of government, all had a hand, directly or indirectly, in the drafting of that immortal document.

Yet a study of that assembly reveals that the authors of the American Constitution were little concerned about emitting theoretical declarations to impress future generations. What history would think of them does not seem to have had much weight. It was an assembly of representatives, each of whom tried to make the opinions of his electors prevail.

The result was an endless series of compromises under which Virginia accepted the bourgeois declaration of the rights of man, insisted on by Massachusetts from the beginning, but only on condition that the Federation would authorize the free importation of slaves.

It may be safely asserted that if the traffic in human flesh was repulsive to the Puritans of Boston, the incorporation in the Constitution of such principles as the equality of man and universal suffrage was unpalatable and seemed absurd to the fine gentlemen of Jamestown.

Both groups found themselves faced by the alternative of compromising or seeing their country disappear from the ranks of independent nations. They compromised, and in so doing, endowed their own country, and indirectly the whole world, with what may be called the democratic tradition.

But for the very reason that it was a democratic work they carried out, not one of the representatives of the States at the constituent assembly yielded on the points deemed essential by his electorate. They compromised, but they did not weaken. Thus each State was enabled to develop along natural lines, along paths different from those taken by the others. A real federation of autonomous states was formed in which, under the liberal principle that the individual should surrender a minimum of his prerogatives and rights to the State, the local entities vested minimum authority in the central power.

Gradually the requirements of practical existence and the benefits of experience made the states, so jealous of their sovereignty, less exacting in their opposition to full unity. This doubtless will be the course pursued by all the free peoples of the world in attaining union, and undoubtedly is the one being followed for the establishment of the Federation of American Nations.

Nevertheless, in the United States this masterpiece of practical politics bore within itself the germ of disintegration, which, after seventy years of growth, was destined to menace the very existence of that democratic nation.

About the middle of the last century, the fight between the ostensible champions of State rights versus the Federal Power came to a head. The struggle was between the defenders of economic privilege and those convinced that certain basic principles had to be respected by all the members of the federal covenant.

Slavery was the catalytic agent that set in motion these antagonistic forces. The clash between them, when it came, gave rise to the bloodiest war until then witnessed by the Western World; the War of Secession.

The victory won by the abolitionists was destined to bring about transformation of national unity into something permanent and unalterable. The growth in strength of the central power, even after the time that has elapsed, is still a process in continual evolution. At this time the United States is closer to centralism than to yesterday's federalism.

The United States has expanded on a scale, hitherto unprecedented, that has rapidly raised it to the rank of a first class power. All this period of its history is dominated by liberal economic principles that allowed the national wealth to be gradually pre-empted by an increasingly smaller class of the population. The principle of equality of man, in the United States, as in other parts of the world, proved to be an instrument wielded against the weak, who could not be protected precisely because their weakness was a fact legally ignored. The twentieth century must witness the end of this process, which threatened to convert a democratic state, the founder of the greatest democracy on earth, into a plutocracy.

The final issue does not seem to be in doubt for, thanks to democratic principles, the individual destitute of protection in the economic sphere never became an outcast. He continued to elect his rulers, and with the passage of time acquired the conviction that his political existence was dependent on the action of the many. He realized that he possessed a force able to override the small group of the powerful.

Certain factors, which I shall review briefly, contributed to strengthening the democratic ideal in the United States. In the first place, the stream of immigration brought new blood into the Union. The newcomers not only sought economic betterment but bore the spiritual scars of Old World tyranny and brought with them dreams of freedom. An important part also was played by isolation from Europe for more than a century, which permitted growth through concentration of effort on the creation of material wealth, without squandering it on costly standing armies or destructive wars. Agricultural riches and facilities for industrialization, as well as growing culture, have had decisive influence in preserving democracy in the United States. Universal education instituted with resources theretofore unprecedented in the history of teaching, has been a splendid investment yielding magnificent returns.

Lastly, one of the most notable contributions to genuinely democratic feeling in the United States has been woman's active participation in public life.

Conciliatory and tolerant sentiments are characteristic of women, in contrast with the aggressiveness and violence of the masculine temperament. It is she who suffers most from the evil effects of a faulty organization of society, from ignorance and the iniquity of war. This is why woman's influence on education, in favor of temperance, in the effort for international peace, has been truly fervent. Her activity in behalf of social welfare work has been untiring. Her inspiration rather than her actual participation in elections has been a fount of good and of collective justice.

We need not refer to the arguments by which Plato defended woman's spiritual value, or to the romantic viewpoint of the Middle Ages, that made of her a being all purity, virtue and moral worth. Participation by woman in the public life of the United States, because of its good common sense, has helped to eliminate from our civilization inequality and the injustice to which her sex has been subjected in other countries. It has been asserted rightly that a civilization is fundamentally distinguished as such, by the protection imparted under it to the two weaker elements of the community, women and children. From this standpoint, in a few nations of the earth civilization has reached as high a level as in the United States. This is undoubtedly due to the share generously allowed women in public life.

In the diffusion of the Pan-American ideal, private initiative has no champion among men so earnest and active as in women's organizations. It is not unusual to find, even in the smallest communities, a delegation from some Pan-American organization composed entirely of women. In each center of this kind the women take part with vehemence and conviction, with passionate energy. In the United States woman unquestionably is an untiring and active ally of the great ideal to which humanity aspires.

T *Democracy and Dictatorship* · IX

THE DEMOCRATIC SYSTEM OF GOVERNMENT, that early in our century was exalted on every side, declined greatly in prestige subsequent to the first World War.

A strong, well organized drive was directed against democratic institutions, especially after the march on Rome.

Democratic systems of government, so it was alleged, did not meet the demands of modern life because technical advances required government by specialists, the only men fitted to solve wisely the increasingly complex problems of public administration.

An enormous majority of the people, say the opponents of free institutions, are unable to see an inch beyond their own petty local affairs. Their vision does not reach to broad economic policies or to the intricate problems of international life. Although these objections are answerable by saying that in almost all countries the citizens exercise their authority by delegation to others, it is asserted that electors allow themselves to be swayed by impulse, political passion or private or sectional interests. Citizens are the victims of demagogues, hence the mediocrity of their rulers and of their parliaments, from the interminable debates of which nothing constructive ever emerges. It is argued that under the democratic system politics engages the whole attention of the people, monopolizes all efforts and converts party contests into futile struggles.

Its detractors end by saying that Democracy is the kingdom of the incompetent, of the unfit and more especially of the irresponsible. Since their powers are derived from the people, accounts have to be rendered only to the latter, an inaccessible entity.

Dictatorships, on the other hand, establish a disciplined form of government, the opponents of democracy contend. When authority is concentrated in a single individual, he can choose his collaborators without being influenced by political considerations, they argue, and the consequence is an efficient administration of well-trained men with a definite feeling of responsibility, as there is someone who can demand it of them. It is added that decisions can be taken quickly without resorting to those compromises or falling into that indecision which in democracies annihilates the most wholesome initiative. The public monies thus are spent to better advantage, say dictatorship's proponents, citing as proof the great material works and ample programs carried out by the dictatorships in the midst of silence and obedience.

Many of the deficiencies ascribed to democratic systems are in reality faults of man himself and are also found in the dictatorships. The only difference is that while in the former system errors receive wide publicity and are openly criticized and remedied, in the latter they are covered over with a veil of falsehood and terror.

Aside from all this, without claiming that popular governments are free from faults, the charges against them are usually founded on isolated cases, preferably chosen from youthful democracies, in an unfair attempt to generalize.

It is not true, first of all, that the people are unable to understand problems of state. On the contrary, the man in the street, the farmer, the worker, business man, all have a keen practical sense that enables them to see where their real interests lie and how to safeguard them. It is also untrue that technicians have no place in democratic governments. The experience of many countries is proof to the contrary, and if at times untrained individuals momentarily gain public power, in the long run the only ones who triumph are those who really show themselves worthwhile.

To think that electors do not call on their representatives to render accounts is merely to fail to see the picture as a whole. The people, when forcibly showing disapproval, sometimes go to such lengths as to slay those who abuse their trust, but in well organized democracies they are more usually content to relegate them to obscurity and oblivion.

Those great material works so noisily vaunted by the dictatorships are not exclusively an attribute of the latter. It is hardly necessary to mention all those which have been carried out by democracies for the good of the community, and not to the glory of the tyrant. Merely recall that the monuments bequeathed to us by classical antiquity, in the Athenian Republic, were not excelled by France under Louis XV. The material grandeur of the mighty American democracy has not been surpassed either by Germany under Hitler or by Italy under Mussolini.

It is not claimed that there are no such things as sinecures, subsidies, abuses and graft in popular governments. But there is no doubt that these vices are commoner under dictatorships, although usually more likely to pass unnoticed at the time committed. They begat the French Revolution, and men like Otto Strasser, who witnessed the inside history of the Nazi regime, have furnished undeniable proofs of the corruption among the leaders of the Third Reich. In contrast, such corruption has been almost non-existent in Switzerland, Norway, Sweden, Denmark or Holland.

One of Democracy's great advantages is that it is in itself an excellent school. It places public affairs, directly or indirectly, in the hands of the really interested parties and thus serves to train the people in political, social and economic matters. Besides, it is a splendid moderating influence, that secures peace, order and progress. When democracy is effective, the people need no armed uprisings to change their rulers or to amend their laws. While the errors of dictatorship can be destroyed only by revolution, without assurance that they will be remedied, the errors of democracy can be corrected peacefully.

A democracy is good not because it makes no mistakes; it does make them, like any other institution which is the work of man. It is good because it can remedy them by peaceful means.

The great power of criticism in the democracies is what constantly purifies them. The representative assemblies may not be efficient, but it is precisely their function of permitting the expression of criticism and disapproval that brings about the conflict of ideas, disseminated and clarified by the best elements among the press, and the altering of enlightened public opinion. Thus the permanent triumph of political wrongdoing against the clear objectives of the common interest is made impossible. It is not the executive power of democratic assemblies—and I refer to bona fide assemblies, not those infected with servility—which is important, but its deliberative power, which provides the ozone of the political atmosphere.

Efficiency is not so much the characteristic feature of democracy as justice and liberty. It is the only system that guarantees the dignity of man and the values of the spirit. Within it all religions, all ideas, all political parties can find a place. It is the only system under which man can live free from the worry and anxiety caused at every moment of existence by the tremendous powers vested in a single individual whose authority is exempt from revision by the people.

However, it must be admitted that the attacks made on democracy after the First World War were attributable to the conduct of its leaders. When this war comes to an end, revision of democratic systems is going to be necessary. Their defects will have to be corrected; popular representation will have to be made more genuine; rulers will have to be more attentive to the will of the people; and the executive power will have to be granted increased authority in times of emergency. Democracy is a system in process of being perfected.

The First World War came to an end under the banner of democratic victory. The whole world anxiously awaited the coming of the new reign of liberty and collective justice. But it was right after the democratic peace that democracy suffered the worst distortions.

We already have analyzed the terrible phenomena attending the rise of imperialism, social injustice and speculation.

Wrongly inspired national and international economic policies brought about a tremendous disorganization and the impoverishment of all the peoples of the earth. This disarrangement and confusion, this incapacity to provide ways and means for reconstruction and emergence from the moral and physical ruin in which those peoples were left after the Great War, culminated in the catastrophic crisis of 1929. Violent economic depression plunged into despair those countries that had for a moment trusted in democratic doctrines. Misery and destitution do not provide an atmosphere in which democratic principles may flourish. Those feelings of tolerance, of mutual respect, of voluntary obedience, which are essential to the practice of true democracy, find it difficult to withstand the reactions of despair and suffering of the masses.

While, on the one hand, poverty grew apace in the democracies and among the peoples that placed their trust in those principles, on the other, the dictatorships, that promised the starving and disillusioned peoples work and prosperity in exchange for liberties, built up the formidable equipment for the next war. For this they used the metals, the raw materials and the credits that the democracies themselves furnished to keep alive the muddy stream of profits and greed.

It is not surprising, therefore, that the enthusiasm of the peoples for adopting democratic constitutions right after the Versailles Treaty was as great as their subsequent disappointment; or that all the countries lacking sound democratic traditions fell into the hands of demagogues promising panaceas for their sufferings. Germany, Italy, Hungary, Austria, Bulgaria were all led to believe that the widespread corruption after World War I and the 1929 economic crisis were the consequence of democracy. Came then the different colored-shirt movements; youth was regimented, and all this courting of Fascist and Nazi institutions resulted in binding the peoples to the chariot wheels of the dictators.

What is astounding is that the peoples accustomed to the democratic way of life did not lose faith in their free institutions. These peoples continued to be just as democratic in 1939 as at the beginning of the century.

Black Shirts fizzled out in England; the Cagoulards in France merely provided amusement; Rexism in Belgium never got beyond a grotesque masquerade; National Action in Switzerland, thanks to the liberty existing in democratic nations, enjoyed only a brief life of contemptible exploitation. Nowhere in the Americas did such attempts achieve any appreciable organization.

For democracy possesses intrinsic worth which lies not only in its being a political system, but in its being a philosophy of life. A fundamental characteristic of the democracies is that they entrust all social values to the individual on the basis of the rights of man face to face with the State.

Before the advent of democratic ideas, this concept was completely ignored, just as it is by the totalitarian systems today. Birth within a caste, inclusion in the Domesday Book of landed estates, being the child of an aristocrat or of a bricklayer, determined privileges and obligations sanctioned by the State, in the face of which the sacred rights of the individual had no validity at all. Exactly the same thing happens in our day; in totalitarian philosophy membership in a class or party bestows rights and obligations quite apart from and superior to the rights of man as an individual.

But the individual continues to be the concern of true democracy. Broadly speaking, this implies that every man, as such, is *ipso facto* entitled to the pursuit of happiness. The man of the people, the common man, the man in the street cannot be cut off from these opportunities. This aim was perverted by classical liberal democracy, which converted the right of the immense majority into an empty formula. Now, however, it is of enormous importance to the onward march of the governments. The State assumes the duty of extending to every man, however humble he may be, economic security, protection against the ills of adversity and the enjoyment of decent living conditions.

To this end the community, which is the aggregate of all its separate components for the mutual good, has grown in power to repel all those attempting to encroach upon individual rights, which singly would be powerless to defend themselves. Hence the enormous strength of collective organizations in modern times.

Man, left to himself, striving singly, was turned over to the mercies of individual units stronger than he. On the other hand, the worker, enrolled in a labor union, has nothing to fear from his employer. The farmer, in an agricultural cooperative, can defy the financial power of the monopolist. A union of small landholders can fight any coalition unjustly threatening the economic rights of each one of them. The basic and essentially democratic fact, however, is that the sole aim of all these organizations is to safeguard the human dignity of their members, their right to well being and the enjoyment of their liberties.

In contrast, the totalitarian theory asserts that in life there are no realities except nations, groups, and peoples; that individuals as such never constitute a reality in social existence. Few assertions contain a more self-evident falsehood. The truth is that the only active and living entity able to feel and suffer, is the individual, man himself; he, therefore, is the ultimate subject of all true rights and duties.

Arbitrary creation of an objective entity, such as a community, a race or a people, is only a pretext wielded by totalitarian philosophies to subordinate the individual to a myth, to other and stronger powers. This means sacrificing human liberties, dignity and spiritual values.

Subjection of the individual to the rights and interests of the community always has been the aim and underlying motive of all organized systems of government. This subordination is substantially recognized by democracies that base their strength on the will of the majority. But majorities composed of individuals can never conspire against themselves, or bargain away the rights of each man and of each individual, inasmuch as opinion is gradually wrought by the free will of each member of the community. However, when such subordination of the individual to the common interest falls into the hands of totalitarian advocates, things are quite different. Then it means cancellation of all individual will; authority once disconnected from the will of the people, subordination is no longer to the community but to the men who have seized the reins of power.

Every attempt to suppress some liberty, is justified in "the good of the people"—their economic and material welfare. Totalitarianism claims that its methods have done away with disorder and unfair distribution of wealth. But the fact is that they start out with a still grosser iniquity, which is the unfair distribution of power. The destinies of man and things lie in the way power is organized. This is why man's basic problem is not solely access to the good things of this life, but —much more important—the manner in which such access is to be obtained. The way in which authority is to be distributed for attainment of this end is just as important as the aim itself.

The social issue is posed between two notions of the State —the totalitarian and the liberal. These concepts are synthesis and antithesis and are destined on the morrow to be merged, within an advancing dialectic, into a combination that will, although preserving certain features of the liberal State, also adopt certain aspects of the collective or totalitarian State.

In the twenty-five planks of the Nazi and Fascist platforms some of the aims stated are those advocated by the democracies; that the State shall see to economic security of the citizens, by guaranteeing employment and social insurance; agrarian reform and defense against industrial monopoly. In actual practice, under Nazi and Fascist regimes, the workers are constantly subjected to an extensive program of athletics, sports, recreation and material benefits. But these measures have only one essential aim; to keep the workers subject to a discipline that makes the men in power invulnerable and which reduces the individuals making up the people to the status of mere automata, deprived of all the rights of human dignity and liberty, without which human happiness cannot find permanent expression.

The achievement of these material gains is based wholly on compulsion and blind obedience to unassailable hierarchical authorities. The subtlest and most ingenious devices have been introduced to maintain this new form of slavery. The small farmer has to keep a work book in which he enters his most trifling activities. These include the place, time and kind of work done, his habits and daily doings, and his acts of loyalty. These entries are not intended for the preparation of some new law, in the drafting of which he has no part, but for the good of a party on whose authority no bounds are set, for a sacred and all-powerful leader. That same farmer may not move elsewhere, or change his occupation, without consent of the authorities, who watch every step he takes and who are, as it were, the hierarchical embodiment of the whole system.

That work-book is the iron fetters of enslavement. Every man who fails to obey is headed for prison, starvation, ostracism, and hasn't the slightest opportunity to escape to freedom in other lands. He is there, he is told, to serve the ends of the State, without answering back. And who is the State? The leader and his henchmen.

Under this regimentation no individual or collective liberties can survive. Naturally collective bargaining, which protects the workers, is outlawed. A series of checks and controls makes the workers powerless by depriving them of the right to choose the place or the kind of labor they prefer. That new way of shackling lives, the work-book, has no other aim than to show that the bearer is a devoted, loyal and unconditional servant of the Fuehrer and of the Nazi Party.

Without the permission of the Labor Bureau no worker can

cherish the hope of bettering himself. By always invoking the interests of the State, labor contracts can be amended, the nature and place of employment changed, without taking into account the desires of the workers at all.

The employer is the labor leader, and if workers do have some right to supervise and determine working conditions, it is only to subordinate the whole policy of production to the supreme arbiter of all, the Nazi party.

Unemployment has been done away with, but at the price of conscripted labor, increased working hours and the forfeiture of every shred of liberty.

It need hardly be said that freedom of thought or belief is outlawed from these slave camps.

Democracy and totalitarian dictatorship, therefore, are two irreconcilable doctrines, locked in a fight to the death. The democracies defend the happiness, peace, and work of the man of the people, of the common man who goes along the streets and roads on his way to the shop, to the fields, to the factory, later to return home where his wife and children are waiting for him.

Democracy is imbued with a fellow-feeling for humanity and looks upon each separate soul, with its hopes and sufferings, as an end in itself. Free institutions overflow with warmest sympathy for the pain of every man. This is why war, which is a source of sacrifice and destruction, of suffering and death, is combated and anathematized by the democracies. Humanity's longing for peace is to them the essence of their philosophy, the objective of their international effort.

Conversely, under Nazism, with its totalitarian doctrines, the State is raised to the rank of a god. Any hindrances in the way of its greatness and dominance are overridden as contemptible. Man passes away but the State is eternal. As man must die, his greatest glory lies in meeting his end fighting for the immortality of the State. Freedom, human dignity, life itself, are but insignificant and transient considerations compared to the existence, the glory and the supremacy of the State. Such a principle is cruel and inhuman. Its philosophy is aggressive. War is glorious and dreams of peace cherished by men of good will are a godsend to the advocates of armed contest, because they will find their foes unprepared.

There is no common ground on which these two doctrines can meet. There is no possible compromise. The fight will continue after insincere truces, until one or the other of the combatants shall win the final victory.

Hence it follows that what constitutes a basic desideratum for the peoples of the Americas—i.e., respect for human liberty, as the groundwork of the domestic policy of the democratic peoples—necessarily becomes a rule of conduct that, flowing over frontiers, determines foreign policy.

No government can practice democracy at home and its antithesis in international dealings. If it craves equality for its own people it must logically want it for the other nations. Accustomed to respecting the opinions of others, even of its adversaries, it has no difficulty in obtaining that respect of others. It has learned from its own experience that if life is a struggle, it can be a contest of ideas, not necessarily of arms. It does not look upon discussion as an insult to its sovereignty, and it is accustomed to relinquishing power when defeated by the popular vote; it knows how to adjust its will to world needs in the interest of harmony among the peoples.

All this leads them to pursue policies of peace, co-operation and concord.

Hence it follows that democratic States are the ones most willingly resorting to conciliations, arbitration and judicial award. It also follows that none is more anxious to see the life of the nations unfold on a plane of universal collaboration.

While Fascism and Nazism embodied in their domestic policies the destruction of the League of Nations and showered invective upon it, the democratic States, on the contrary, strove at all times to strengthen that institution.

In democractic States war is not an issue left to the will of one man. Our constitutions require that so weighty a decision receive the approval of Congress or Parliament. Peoples are naturally peaceful, and when they resort to war, or wage it under the compulsion of their leaders, vested with tremendous and dictatorial powers, or in lawful self-defense, they know that they have nothing at all to gain from war, unless it be, in Winston Churchill's admirable words, "Blood, sweat and tears."

T

HE DEMOCRATIC SYSTEM DID NOT COME INTO being in the Ibero-American countries under such favorable signs as in the United States, where all the elements were at hand for the development of an autonomous civilization and the agricultural and industrial potentialities for its subsequent growth.

The United States was settled by men cradled in the tradition of English liberties. Many were deeply religious, and came to the new country in search of the freedom of worship they were denied in their native land.

Tocqueville, in his *Democracy in America*, which still preserves the freshness, the penetration and the enthusiasm of the day in which it was written –1833–, dazzled by the imposing sight that was the United States, speaks in brilliant pages of the birth of a democracy "the like of which the ancient world had never dared imagine." Government by representative assembly, that powerful leaven of all free institutions, was of long standing in the English system. The very dogma that power resides in the people had brilliant advocates in the reign of the Tudors.

The democratic system and the early representative assemblies were the seed from which the present great American democracy sprang. Moreover, as has already been said, the fathers of independence were men of highest attainments, many of whom were admired not only in their own country and the other colonies, but in England itself; among them were Jefferson, Hamilton, Jay, Madison, and Adams.

As a result, the first steps of the United States as an independent nation were guided by a system, a democratic method rooted in the experience of several centuries of free government as colonies.

The contrast between this favored situation of the United States and that of the Ibero-American countries is profound. The *conquistadores* came to our shores in search of adventure and easy wealth; their greed led them to enslave the natives. From the beginning the word "liberty" was proscribed in the lands they had conquered. The phrase of one of the last vice-roys, the Marquis of Lacroix, is famous: "It is well that the vassals of the great monarch who occupies the throne of Spain should know once and for all that they were born to hold their tongues and obey, not to discuss matters of state policy." The result was that the Ibero-American nations had no opportunity whatever to learn the lessons of liberty by practicing them. So it is not surprising that when they achieved their independence, having no training or preparation, each acted according to its own lights.

To be sure, Hidalgo and some of his associates who headed the movement for freedom in Mexico had read Montesquieu and the leading encyclopedists. Bolívar had read the classics of ancient Rome and of England. But none had the solid, systematic background needed to lay the foundations of an enduring democracy and, above all, none had a people ready to receive the democratic doctrines. This led to the trial-and-error methods, the strange artificialities, the contradictory improvisations, the daring experiments, such as the short-lived empire of Iturbide, the periodical returns to absolutism and the uninterrupted struggle between the new ideas, unable as yet to make themselves clear, and the despotic spirit of the epoch. It was a period of disorders, *coups d'etat,* and barely-disguised anarchy, during which the countries swung back and forth between federated and centralized forms of government.

Side by side with this went the poverty inherited from the colonial system, which had created neither the small land-owner nor a middle class, nor an elementary culture, so that there were no existing institutions to support any of the attempts to create democratic standards. These standards can-not flourish in abject poverty and ignorance. A certain eco-nomic security is an indispensable basis for the enjoyment of human liberty, just as is education. Under a government designed for all, the economic and cultural capacity to play their part in government must be had by all.

It is easy to see how many handicaps Latin America has had to overcome in its attempts to build up free institutions. In the century and a half of independent life, these countries have had to do away with conditions incompatible with the existence and exercise of democracy.

Just as the United States had to fight one of the bloodiest of civil wars to abolish slavery, the Latin American nations have had to destroy the organic bases of despotism. It is unintelligent to inveigh against the democratic systems of Latin America. The truth is that democracy has never existed in these countries, largely because a feudal system has continued there, under the control of a small group of the descendants of the colonial gentry, masters of the wealth and resources of the nation.

The citizens who play the most important role in a real democracy—that is to say, the enlightened majority capable of understanding the national problems—do not exist there. With slight differences the democratic process has been falsified throughout Latin America.

In the earlier stages of this process it is the general, the Prætorian Guard type, self-seeking, ambitious, short-sighted, who rules over sections of the country with a certain autonomy, and on occasion scales the post of highest authority. He is a restless, almost legendary type, who lives for adventure, without program or principles.

Next in the scale is the *caudillo,* the chieftain. The *caudillo* is nearly always a general, rarely a civilian, having a vision of the whole, capable of formulating programs and political platforms. His distinguishing trait is to put himself beyond existing institutions even though these have been created and sanctioned by advanced laws upholding liberty and democracy. The *caudillo* is above these laws. He governs without being responsible in any way, and often when his direct powers terminate, he exercises his will through intermediaries, friends he can depend upon, pulling the wires behind the scenes. In his study on American democracies, García Calderón reached the conclusion that the influence of each of these *caudillos* in Latin America generally covers an average span of twenty years.

But gradually the culture of the people, the pride of the people, demands that the president chosen be the one who governs. And as this feeling that the first duty of a president is to be president grows stronger in the responsible members of the government, the democratic process moves up a step. The president becomes the voice of the people.

This condition has not yet come about in all the countries of Latin America. Nor is this evolutionary process the clearest proof of the validity of institutions. Once the president chosen by the people has assumed the responsibility of office a new concentration is necessary: the submission of the presidential power in accordance with constitutional law, and assemblies, representative of the people and to the courts.

The characteristic feature of the Latin American governmental set-up is that the president is everything; he is the country, he is the supreme power. In contrast to countries having a parliamentary regime, his ministers are but a pallid reflection of himself. He governs, the assembly obeys. This situation is aggravated by the fact that the people going through this stage of democratic evolution take no part in the election of their representatives.

Many different systems, but all corrupt, make the election of representatives and senators mere empty formulas, mechanisms of fraud, which render these elections meaningless and deprive them of authority and power. In contrast, the election of the president in almost all the Latin American countries is characterized by the real interest of the people in this choice. All the force of public opinion built up during the preceding years of government, in which the people lacked any share in the appointment of officials and the carrying out of political programs, makes itself felt on this occasion. The presidential choice is violent, impassioned, seething with genuine interest for the people. This is why at the time of presidential elections in Latin America, there often are riots, military coups and real revolutions.

This phenomenon, which has occurred repeatedly throughout the history of the Latin American countries since independence, reveals the amazing uniformity among our different nationalities and the profound contrast with the parliamentary systems of Europe. There the public puts all its force, interest and civic sense into the parliamentary elections. It is also in marked contrast to the presidential elections of the United States.

From its inception, the government of the United States entered upon the highest plane of the democratic process. Moreover, in the United States the president, "elected by [direct] popular vote is more a spokesman of the people" than is the president of France, who is "a guest in the Palais de l'Elysée"; but unquestionably in the United States the system of checks and balances so admirably embodied in its institutions acts as a limitation on the executive power. The legislative and judicial departments of the federal government, as well as the individual states, are forces which always keep the action of the president within its strictly constitutional limits.

There is one conquest all the Latin American countries have made which serves as a brake against the embattled tyrannies and the dictatorial aspirations to indefinite terms of office, and that is the no-re-election proviso. With certain variations this has been written into all our constitutions and, when carried out, it is an effective barrier to unlimited term of office and an aid to the transformation of the *caudillo* into the president of the nation.

Unfortunately this guarantee of free institutions, of the evolution toward real freedom and a democratic way of life, is often evaded and violated, delaying Latin America's advance toward democracy.

These transgressions of the law are unquestionably due to the lack of enlightened and organized public opinion. The law must be linked to public opinion through the creation of genuinely free parties. The formation of valid parties, enjoying all their constitutional rights, will be the guarantee of the development and strength of democratic institutions for the future.

Without a fearless and enlightened public opinion, without well-organized political parties which are aware of their civic responsibility in the exercise of their powers, the democratic statutes are but an empty shadow.

Let us examine in detail the characteristics of the progress toward democracy in certain of the American countries.

In Mexico it was not until the Constitution of 1857 that an organized and almost perfect attempt was made in the direction of liberty and self-government. Democracy at that moment had real champions such as Otero and Arriaga. The Magna Charta of the Mexican liberal party formulated the bases of the democratic system, guaranteeing the rights of man and the exercise of political powers.

From that time on the struggle was to make the existence of this democracy a reality. It was necessary to curb three factors inimical to freedom: the church, which controlled the political and economic life of the country; the owners of large landed estates, or *latifundia,* whose power was based on an unjust distribution of the land; and the army, which put the government at the mercy of military insurrections and *coups d'etat,* and made democracy a tragic farce.

The achievements of Mexico under its revolutionary governments are of the greatest value, because they mark the evolution of the country's institutions to the point of almost achieving their democratic aims.

To appreciate the boldness of the measures outlined by the Constitutional Convention with regard to the church, one must imagine the state of mind of the masses in that day. They were the victims of a fanaticism which confused the clergy with religion and the property of the convents and the bishops with divinity itself. The secularization of the enormous possessions of the church, which was the greatest landowner of the country, and the subsequent decisions separating church and state, served as the basis not only for the economic rehabilitation of Mexico, but was one of the most important contributing factors to the freedom of conscience, without which no civilization is worthy of the name.

The agrarian reforms are equally significant. These received legal sanction in the Constitution of 1917. At present it may be said that this reform is approaching its final stage. In the last twenty-five years more than 61,750,000 acres have been converted into collective or small individual holdings, more than a quarter of the arable land of the republic. Grants of land have been made to about a million and a half peasants, or to about half the rural population of Mexico.

The International Labor Office, a subsidiary of the League of Nations, published in 1937 a carefully documented study in which it said:

"As producers and consumers, all the new landholders [of Mexico] are gradually entering into a new rural society, in which they are called to play a role that will enable them to fulfil their own destinies more freely and become an element of positive usefulness to the whole community. Wage-paid labour has ceased to be the dominant factor in rural life; the emancipation of the *peón* has largely been achieved in what, all things considered, has been a rapid cycle, and the violent contrasts of the past between traditional wealth and traditional pauperism are being abolished by a change of attitude towards, and an understanding of, the Indian and *mestizo* rural inhabitants of the country, who have been discovered to be human beings. Thanks to State action, in the future better living conditions and an increased income will be enjoyed by each rural family."

Concurrent with agrarian reform, it was necessary to deal with the labor problem in the same spirit of justice and equity. The bases of this were outlined in the 1917 Constitution.

Thanks to these measures, Mexico now has a labor legislation that has been gradually becoming a reality, and which ranks among the fairest and most advanced of the world. It was inevitable that Mexico's measures to protect the rights of her workers and farmers should have brought her into conflict with powerful international corporations. But the justifiable attitude of the Mexican state has won it the respect and approval of America's leaders, and is in keeping with the conscience and trend of events in the whole world.

It also was necessary to do away with the militarism which constituted an insurmountable barrier to the democratic way of life. The dearly-won gains and conquests on the path of progress had to be protected from military coups and the attacks and ambitions of armed factions, so that the government of the country could really represent the free expression of the will of the majority. To this end the army, which had been a special caste within the state, was democratized and converted into the anonymous defender of the nation's institutions. Its mission as guardian of the integrity and safety of the Republic was emphasized.

The time has not come to assert that the difficult last stage of democratic life has been definitely achieved. But there is no gainsaying that the civil masses and the Mexican army jointly aspire to separate the armed forces from all political activity and ambitions, the unmistakable hallmark of free institutions. When this has been accomplished, the honor of the army will be elevated along with the liberties and dignity of the Republic. The inauguration of compulsory military service will contribute greatly to the strengthening of the democratic spirit and system in Mexico.

These three campaigns I have outlined, which are integrated with the education and constant betterment of the people, form the backbone of the revolutionary and progressive achievements of Mexico and constitute its true contribution to democracy. This contribution has been of the greatest importance, particularly for the life of free institutions in Latin America, all of which have lived, for the most part, under the same conditions and difficulties as the Mexican Republic. Mexico has been, in many respects, an example, a standard and a guide.

In the Argentine, although the causes were different, the results were in a measure similar to those we have pointed out in the United States. There Spanish colonization was much more homogeneous; there were no religious differences or important class rivalries. Exploitation on the basis of large colonial land grants was of brief duration and, thanks to the country's agricultural wealth, better bases existed for democratic experiments.

The Spaniards and, later on, the Creoles, were in almost complete control, for the aborigines, Charrúas, Terandíes, Maradíes, Patagonians, etc., lived in a primitive state. Having kept their racial unity all through the epoch of Spanish domination, the Argentinans acquired a sense of their own power in their struggles with the English, and their emancipation from Spain was one of the quickest and least bloody of all America.

This was not the case, however, with respect to national unity, for the struggle that broke out in nearly all our countries between the supporters of a federal versus a centralized form of government filled a long period of the Argentine's history.

The process of converting the country into a democracy became entangled in the struggle between Buenos Aires, which attempted to assume the leadership, and the provinces. Fortunately a spirit of conciliation prevailed, and thanks to the leadership of brilliant and patriotic statesmen and a wise immigration policy, the Argentine Republic has become, taking into account the relativity of human accomplishments, one of the most firmly united countries on our continent.

The right to oppress defeated opponents did not accrue to the victors; traditionalist parties have rotated in power and the electoral machinery, with brief interruptions, has functioned normally.

That Colombia is one of the most democratic nations of South America is due to a variety of reasons. The patriarchal organization that prevailed among the native groups, and the fact that the conqueror of Colombia, Gonzalo Jiménez de Quesada, was a lawyer, would seem to have been influential factors in creating the respect the Colombians feel and practice toward their institutions.

The history of Colombia after it had won its independence reveals an almost complete absence of military events which might have enhanced the personality of the leaders of the armed forces.

The number of generals and *caudillos* has been much smaller there than in many other countries of America. Even during the frequent civil wars and insurrections occurring since its independence, the leaders of these have distinguished themselves more for their political achievements than for their feats of arms.

The case of General Santander is an example. The Colombians regard him as one of the persons who did most to consolidate the political structure of the country, and they call him "The Man of Law." Nevertheless, if one analyzes the statesmanship of this president of Colombia, one comes to the conclusion that he established principles rather than laws. For him it was important that the legislation and the government of a country be in harmony with its own particular characteristics. Bolívar, the Liberator, was his inspiration. His guiding purpose was to set up a strong, solid government.

Thus it was possible for the people of Colombia, without endangering the fundamental principle of the rights of man, to avoid those obstacles in the path of political organization which beset the beginning of independence everywhere.

The democratic ideas of the Colombian nation have developed around this basic concept of individual guarantees. Respect for these guarantees has been one of the chief traits of the inhabitants of the former New Granada. Only in sporadic cases did their civil wars occasion the violation of these rights, and all their internal struggles have been characterized by a deep respect for human life and dignity. Thus General Mosquera, who led a *coup d'etat* and put several members of Congress under arrest, was deposed and tried by the legislature and sentenced to two years of prison for his attempt to make himself dictator, a sentence subsequently commuted to two years of exile.

This respect of the people of Colombia for the rights of man is both a product of its culture and a bulwark against autocratic forms of government.

These observations regarding the United States, Mexico, Argentina and Colombia give us an idea of what has happened in the other republics of America. By taking into account their geographical location, their racial composition, their historical background, we can easily tell to which group they belong.

In all of them the democratic impulse has been irresistible. It is superfluous to go into details of how the system of popular government has evolved in each. The experiments in parliamentary methods in Chile, its strong civic sense and its latest elections; the new constitution of Cuba; the deep-seated sense of equality of Brazil; the political changes in Ecuador; the culture of Uruguay, which makes it a model of institutional organization; the continuance in power of the traditional parties in Peru and Venezuela, in Bolivia and Paraguay; the democratic aspirations which manifest themselves so strongly in certain regions of Central America—notably Costa Rica—are clear proof that in our continent the future of government of the people, by the people and for the people grows steadily brighter.

Several different factors are necessary for its complete realization: a more intensive program of public education; the economic improvement of the condition of workers and farmers; the development of better means of communication; encouragement of immigration; and the adoption of social and sanitary measures. But, above all, the most powerful stimulus to the rapid realization of the democratic ideal in all these countries will be the prestige the democracies will achieve by their triumph over the totalitarian states and the consolidation of the ideal of Pan Americanism.

The mere comparison between the present and the past, with its uprisings, conspiracies, and sinister and shameless personal ambitions, reveals an upward march.

Moreover, who can hold back the progress of a nation? Who can deny that the increasing pace of the communication of thought, which outdistances space, is a factor that strengthens the public opinion of a country and makes it the architect of its own fate?

We have fought as President Avila Camacho of Mexico puts it, for "a better man and a better democracy in a better world" and we shall not answer the challenge of the future with slavery and despotism.

It is not for nothing that in every one of our nations, every day and every step of this war, the words on which free institutions are based have been echoing in our ears.

There is great poverty in America. The union of all our countries will build economic security for all. There is great ignorance in the masses of our people. The union of all the nations of America, the reciprocal influences of our civilizations, our material progress will every day further dissipate the ignorance of the multitudes.

In many of our countries the phrase "free institutions" is a misleading term. We have dictatorships—some enlightened, serving as bridges between the die-hard elements and the coming of free democracy; others, frankly reactionary—but none of them will endure. The overwhelming sentiment in favor of human liberty, as a result of the democratic triumphs won at the price of such great suffering and so many lives heroically sacrificed, will make the will of the people for free government invincible. And in our America the ever-growing propaganda for democracies will be a decisive force, as will the example ot nations that are ruled by genuinely democratic standards, and the expanding organization of the masses to exercise their rights and live in social justice.

The ideal of the continent will be carried to fulfillment under the solemn covenant of solidarity between free peoples, from which the twin tyrannies of despotism and human subjection will be eliminated. This means that one-man rule, the tradition of sinister dictatorship, the shocking militarism that has befouled our history for centuries, will not be able to endure under the emblem of the victorious democracies.

The democratic ideal, instead of standing in the way of the unity of America, is an incentive, a hope, a tower of strength, a column of fire.

I
Culture and Race · XI

IN OUR DISCUSSION AGAINST IMPERIALISM AND THE dictatorial regimes still surviving in the continent, we have refuted the argument most flaunted that they are obstacles to the possibility of union among the American peoples.

Now let us examine another of the most weighty objections, the difference of culture and race among these nations. Men of little faith maintain that the practical, realistic, creative spirit of the Anglo-Saxon is incompatible with the verbose, declamatory, fruitless idealism of the Latin-American. The latter—they say—because of his Spanish heritage, is rashly quixotic, impatient of the historic expediency of compromise and conciliation. Enamoured of sentimental principles, he does not hesitate to sacrifice the destiny of his country for them. In a practical world he spends his life reciting absolute postulates, with the result that his political action, without roots in enduring interests, veers this way and that, lacks historic continuity, and the high idealism of his principles, and having no support in reality, gives way to government by the strongest and to bastard ambitions. The democratic struggle, based on tolerance and compromise, turns into insolent and aggressive exhibitionism. Stubborn individualism is the law of these peoples of Iberian extraction. No one can deny their vital impulse, their adventurous spirit, capable of great undertakings, great enthusiasm. But these qualities lack co-ordinating force, a vertebral column, and they express themselves in positive explosions, in contradictory attitudes, ineffectual because of their lack of coherence and organization.

Thus out of this traditional, hereditary anarchy, the Latin American republics have been developing into restless so-called democracies, unable to cultivate the virtues of law and order. Their easily offended egoism stands in the way of solidarity. So, on the one hand, we have the Ibero-Americans, with their brilliant intellectual gifts and their shortcomings in the realm of action, pursuing their troubled progress, torn by constant contradictions, unable to consolidate either their democratic principles or their material well-being. On the other hand, we have the United States, whose highly developed spirit of association and indomitable energy, always pursuing the continuity of national aims despite changes in the political parties in power, has been able to create not only a splendid material civilization, but one of the world's most authentic and efficient democracies.

In his book, *The Future of Latin America*, Manual Ugarte discusses the formation of our democracies, their ethnic composition, that corrosive personal ambition which plays so important a role in our politics, the empty verbosity of our teaching, the sloth, the envy, the thirst for power, and the lack of moral feeling, which many thoughtful writers have observed in the Latin-American. Nevertheless, after analyzing all these writers, such as Zumeta, Bulnes, Blanco-Fombona, Oliveira Lima, he ends his study with high hopes for the future of these American nations. He puts his faith in the American that will emerge from the fusion of all the races on this continent, who will slough off these vices to become a synthesis of the virtues of the different races.

In reality, the true motive for our faith in the future American rests on the fact that all the vices attributed to the Latin-American are not innate but a consequence of the abject poverty in which the masses live there, their lack of equipment, preparation, techniques, and above all, credits, to cope with difficult natural surroundings.

When a man lacks the means to achieve success he sinks into a state of spiritual depression. He is obliged to waste his energy in violent but fruitless efforts, and without faith that his achievements will be lasting. He grows accustomed to violence, he loses the systematic creative endeavor of the victorious races, and he sinks into a slough of doubt and indolence which fosters vices that are not inherent in his nature but the result of his environment and of circumstances too strong for him to combat.

Slavery in any form destroys the spirit and smothers the innate virtues. A real basis for the American's faith in tomorrow is that soon the shackles which bind him will be broken. When his thought and his initiative find the instruments they require to transform themselves into creative action, then his melancholy and arrogance will be replaced by the powerful impulse to create and produce. His lack of respect for the law, which gives him nothing and guarantees him nothing, will be replaced by the determination to defend the institutions which will protect his gains and assure their permanence. His exaggerated sense of self, his individualism which finds no outlet in an atmosphere hedged about by limitations and frustrations, which denies him everything, will be replaced by a sense of the group, in which co-operation brings strength, wealth and prosperity.

In the vast expanse of America there are a few scattered significant examples of the truth of these assertions. Our large cities, Buenos Aires, Rio de Janeiro, Mexico City, all reveal the creative impulse which springs from their own powers. In the Republic of Mexico, near the frontier of the United States, there is the city of Monterrey, having a population of some 200,000. It has been developed by purely Mexican enterprise, work and initiative. Special circumstances have made it possible for the inhabitants of this city to carry on their work with success, and this in turn has stimulated continuing progress. Whoever has visited the state of Yucatán in the southeast of Mexico has seen the fine agricultural civilization that has been created by the whole population of this region which is of pure Mayan race. The circumstance that it has had a market for its vast production of henequen has made possible, thanks to the labor of all under the guidance of men of ability, and despite frequently adverse conditions, the creation of a genuine native prosperity in which any nation could take pride. Examples of this sort are frequent in our countries.

Energy should not be employed in the pursuit of objects which are unattainable or doomed to certain failure, such as attempting to master natural conditions which are too powerful for man. When this happens, energy is frittered away in sterile ventures, in personal conflicts. In a world so ordered that, to live, man must exploit man, selfish individualism is the law. But when it is nature that is to be exploited, association becomes a common objective. The idea of collectivism derives power from the fact that co-operation is in the interest of all.

It is only natural that two worlds as different as the Anglo-Saxon and the Latin-American should have produced differing civilizations. One is characterized by the development of techniques, the creation of an exceptional prosperity, the love of comfort and material well-being. The other, despite privations and difficulties, has made great contributions in the field of intelligence and human sentiment. Its art has achieved forms superior to those of satisfied nations. Individualism, the harsh personal struggle, the romantic thirst for adventure, all tend to foster higher expressions in the field of art. The exchange of these different manifestations of human activity will bring about a fertile integration.

In the Anglo-Saxon civilization, with its emphasis on material well-being, the love of liberty is probably its greatest contribution to mankind's destiny. In the other, born amid poverty and privations, where liberty cannot come to its full flowering (because to do so it would need economic independence), the dream of social justice finds powerful expressions which are also a great force for redemption in the destinies of mankind. For the world has need of the moral strength of the countries which have suffered and have extracted from their suffering universality of thought and grandeur of purpose.

We may be sure that the difference between these civilizations, far from being an obstacle, is a hope and a spiritual treasure for this continent. For what else was the Renaissance than the conjunction of two culturally differing worlds?

Give to the Hispanic Americas the modern technology with which to conquer Nature easily, and we shall see that in all the countries of the continent, men of action, of initiative, and of imagination will step forth, men who will know the same joy of living and working, with the same efficiency, as the best endowed men anywhere.

The first systematic advocate of the theory of racial superiority was the French writer and diplomat, Count Joseph Arthur de Gobineau. Paradoxically enough, he was imbued with the Germanic ideal and also with admiration for the Orient. His influence quickly made itself felt in Germany, where Nietzsche may be considered his follower.

The racial ideas the Hohenzollerns adopted to further their Pan-Germanism were to find a fantastic exponent in Adolf Hitler. He and Rosenberg, National Socialism's philosopher, used them as their banner and distorted them to serve as the basis for the Reich's pretended justification for enslaving all the other peoples of the world.

Hitler in *Mein Kampf* boldly states his belief that all culture, art, science and inventions are the creative product of the Aryan: "He is the Prometheus of humanity, from whose radiant brow the divine spark of genius has always sprung, ever lighting anew the fire, which, in the form of knowledge, has illuminated the night of speechless mysteries and thus has revealed to man the road he should follow to become the master over other beings of this earth. Cause him to disappear, and profound darkness would descend again upon the earth, and in a few centuries human civilization would vanish, and the world would become a desert. . . . We all feel that in some distant future mankind will be confronted with problems that can be solved only by a master nation of the most elevated race which has at its disposal all the means and resources of the whole world."

Such phrases as these recall the opinion of Hitler's racial theories that Trotsky, one of the founders of another type of totalitarianism, stated in July, 1933, shortly after the rise to power of the National Socialist Party. The late Soviet leader called them a fanatical, chauvinistic, and presumptuous manifestation, and pointed out that the leaders of National Socialism were not German. Hitler is an Austrian; Hess, a colonial; and Rosenberg, from the Baltic provinces of the former empire of the Czar.

If the race theory, twisted to suit the ends of the Nazis, is so absurd that it refutes itself, the doctrine of the innate inequalities of the races, as set forth by Gobineau, come off no better when confronted with the irrefutable facts of history.

A descendant of the famous author summed up the gist of the thesis of his essay on the inequality of the human races, considering them as falling into three pure types: the black, essentially emotional; the yellow, materialistic; and the white, productive. Only to the Aryan did he assign the "social sense" and the capacity to "govern socially." His blood preserves the progressive vitality of human society, which declines and dies out when the Aryan blood is diluted with other mixtures. According to Gobineau, it is the Aryan blood which is the dynamic primary cell of civilization.

But Gobineau contradicts himself and at times forgets this rigid division in which he has attempted to confine mankind. In his book *Three Years in Asia,* he describes the Asiatic genius as the fountainhead of intellectual supremacy of the ages to which the world owes all gratitude.

Elie Faure, discussing the basis of Gobineau's theory, brings to light its weakness, using the brilliant style which distinguishes his work:

"In the whole world there is not a single person of 'pure race', assuming that this expression still has any meaning.

"History does not begin except through racial mixing. There is no recorded history before Egypt, unless it be, I believe, the timeless negro culture which came up the valley of the Nile toward the Mediterranean; and that of Asia whence, long ago, the white man descended. There is nothing before the India of the Veddas, that first poetic spark lightened in the souls of the men who lived between the Ganges and the Indus by the dramatic encounter between the calm blue-eyed giant who descended from the mountains, and the black man with fever-bright eyes who came from the lowlands and jungles of Deccan, moving to the rhythm of his songs and dances. The two Greek civilizations would not have existed without the impact between the bronzed fishermen from Asia and Africa and the barbarians who descended from Mt. Pindar to the sea. Nor the Italian, without the expansion of the primitive white tribe which filtered outward among the Semitized and mixed Melanian populations of Southern Italy, Sicily, Africa, Greece, Syria and Spain; nor the French, nor the German, nor those legions of mixed race who rushed down the valley of the Rhone to do battle with the Celts, scattered throughout Gaul, and the Germans, who had to be continually pushed back across the Rhine."

There is no such thing as a pure race. In reality nations are mixtures of different races, that is to say, mixtures of various ethnical mixtures.

The vast stage of history presents the same race as the conqueror of today and the conquered of tomorrow. Brilliant and creative in one period, and, sooner or later, sunk in obscurity. Groups of the same race have produced cultures that are completely different, as the Aryans in India, Iran and Europe. What is there in common between the magnificent life of the Sumerians and the bloody savagery of the tribes of Attila, though both are manifestations of the same Turanian race?

In contrast, the Nahuatl-Mayas in Mexico and the Egyptians in Africa, without the slightest racial connection, produced very similar cultures. In what way is the Byzantine juridical culture inferior to the concepts of European Aryan law?

From earliest times there has been a continual coming and going of peoples, invasions, conquests, wars, migrations; the ebb and flow of cross-breeding and mixtures of the original strains.

The racial mysticism of Gobineau, which would make the destiny of the peoples hinge upon the number of drops of Aryan blood in their veins, becomes meaningless in the light of history.

But if his theory is false, as are all unilateral theories that attempt to explain the evolution of mankind by a single factor, whether it be the geographical determinism of Ratze or the historic materialism of Marx, who conceived race as something fixed once and for all and permanently divided into categories of value, it is nevertheless true that races do exist, i. e., if by that word is meant what, in my opinion, constitutes its real essence: the aggregate of biological, psychological and cultural traits which characterize a human group at a given moment.

There is no such thing as superior races, but there are inferior biological types, some degenerate, others hopelessly deteriorated. One of the most pressing problems which confronts us in America is not that of race, with which we need not concern ourselves, for the matter can be left to natural miscegenation, but that of improving the biological type of each nation. As this need is especially acute in Latin America, it would be well to examine briefly the present condition of the population.

The biological type of the Latin American population is in large part deficient, and in certain instances, actually decadent. The explanation is geographic, also economic and of a sanitary nature.

Among geographic factors two are basic: the climate and latitude.

In certain studies on Sweden, it is said that one of that nation's greatest assets is its geographical position and climate. Animal life is invigorated there; over successive generations, organisms grow stronger and better. Cold climates, if not beyond the powers of human resistance, keep the body cells in a continuous state of struggle and renewal and are an unfavorable medium for epidemics lurking in wait to attack and weaken the organism.

In contrast, countries with a mild climate, and above all in the tropics, require less activity; the cells find heat enough from without, and their function of reproducing energy is slowed down. In addition, a hostile world of uncontrollable epidemics, which proliferate in infinite forms and directions, menace man on all sides.

Doctor Manuel Gamio has made the telling point that latitude is a determining factor in the biological development of peoples. In the far north and south, as in the United States and Argentina, conditions are very favorable, whereas the heat and humidity of the highlands and tropical regions are very harmful to their inhabitants.

A world-renowned authority, Dr. Alexis Carrel, has written on this subject as follows:

"The physical and chemical peculiarities of the climate, the soil and the food can be used as instruments for modifying the individual. Endurance and strength generally develop in countries where seasons are extreme, where mists are frequent and sunlight rare, where hurricanes blow furiously, where the land is poor and sown with rocks. The schools devoted to the formation of a hard and spirited youth should be established in such countries, and not in southern climates where the sun always shines and the temperature is even and warm. Florida and the French Riviera are suitable for weaklings, invalids and old people, or normal individuals in search of a short rest. Moral energy, nervous equilibrium, and organic resistance are increased in children when they are trained to withstand heat and cold, dryness and humidity, burning sun and chilly rain, blizzards and fog—in short, the rigors of the season in northern countries. The resourcefulness and hardiness of the Yankees were probably due, in a certain measure, to the harshness of a climate where, under the sun of Spain, there are Scandinavian winters."

The economic conditions which prevail throughout nearly all Latin America also have had an unwholesome effect on the biological development of our people.

Sparse population and lack of capital have made our countries economically weak. The agricultural and industrial workers are undernourished, their capacity as consumers very scant. As a result there is little circulation of wealth and little stimulus for the development of an integrated economy.

Handicapped by serious hereditary ailments, undernourished and with a standard of living so low they are unable to resist so many evil circumstances, the biological development of the Latin-American masses is, in general, difficult and deficient. Under these conditions, each new generation inherits a constantly lowered physique; there is steady decline. In many regions of Latin America, one is deeply distressed by the state of the population; one cannot but feel a burning desire to help them in time.

Sanitation and hygiene are decisive factors. The general low level of both in Latin America is the cause of the very high infant mortality rate and results in a defective biological type among survivors and descendants.

The countless maladies, some hereditary, some endemic, others epidemic, which beset our population, are of various origins. Some, such as typhoid and dysentery, are caused by the water-supply, in most communities exceedingly bad. Others are of parasitic origin, such as hook-worm. Others are bacterial, such as small-pox and spotted typhus; malaria with its tragic aftermaths—anaemia, cochexia, and as a climax, tuberculosis; and finally syphilis and other venereal diseases, either inherited or contracted.

The diet of great masses of the population of Latin America is extremely deficient, particularly lacking in proteins, fats and the vitamins essential for proper nourishment.

Corn, which, with certain other cereals, has formed the chief alimentary bases of the Indian races on the continent from time immemorial, is a very partial diet, and wholly inadequate as the mainstay, for it does not provide efficacious biological protection under the conditions of modern life.

The lack of proteins and vitamins in the diet makes itself felt in the United States as well as in Latin America, although the former is the best-nourished country in the world. Mr. Claude R. Wickard, Secretary of Agriculture in the United States, in a talk before the opening session of the Second Inter-American Conference, which met in Mexico on July 6, 1942, said, "In the United States we welcome the changes in our agricultural plant which the war has compelled, for we believe the result will be a sounder agricultural economy. Many people of our nation have never eaten enough meat, milk, poultry and fruits. There has been malnutrition, as in every other country of the world.

". . . Home production of protein and vitamin-rich foods assures better nutrition. We have found that malnutrition is as common on the farm as in cities. The answer is increased consumption of fresh vegetables and fruits, meat, eggs and milk products."

Alcoholism is one of the most widespread vices of the American continent and one of the greatest contributing factors to lowering the biological standard of our peoples. In Latin America the alarming proportions it has acquired come from historic and social as well as economic and cultural causes.

From the arrival of Cortez, the conquerors took advantage of the Indian's fondness for intoxicating drinks to dominate him, and fostered and encouraged this natural tendency.

What measures can be taken to do away with this dire enemy of the strength and fitness of our people? A broad campaign to develop an interest in sports, proper diet and an intensive program of education. Mere legal enactments will not produce the desired results, as the Prohibition amendment in the United States clearly proved.

There are few more urgent needs than combating this scourge of humanity. Gladstone's scathing words are still valid: "Alcoholism has caused more disasters in the world than famine, plague and war put together. Famine and plague decimate a people; war kills them; but drunkenness first dishonors them, then transmits its curse and finally destroys them."

I have touched upon all the causes which lead to the degeneration of our race, because no study of the future of America would be complete without them.

In the face of these somber realities, our faith and conviction in the advantages of a union among all the peoples of America to combat their common ills grows and is strengthened.

It becomes as clear as the noon-day sun that unity and mutual trust will make it possible to do with the greatest ease what our separate countries, remote, isolated, and without the necessary resources, could not possibly do by themselves. City and countryside can be made healthful; the plagues of the tropics can be combatted; in a word, the biological strength of America can be built up anew. By the bold, broad use of credits, inside a generation we can rebuild the pristine vigor of our races. Nothing could lend Pan Americanism so much prestige as the co-operation of all our nations, and particularly the United States, which could employ its vast wealth to make available enormous credits to finance a program to fight all the forces that undermine the health and strength of the nations of America. Nothing would be so deeply appreciated and nothing would be easier or better business. In this way, human beings would be restored to capability and efficiency that would enable them to play their part in building up a great civilization.

At the first Inter-American Congress for Indian problems, held in Pátzcuaro, Michoacán, April 14-24, 1940, it was recognized that the problem of the native groups of America is a matter of public interest, continental in scope and bound up with the plans for solidarity among the peoples and governments of the New World:

"The Indians, as descendants of the original inhabitants of America, have a preferential claim on the protection of the public authorities to make up for the deficiencies of their physical and intellectual development. Therefore, whatever is done to improve their condition will be in the nature of an atonement for the neglect they have suffered in the past."

This generous, just and humanitarian proposition is in sharp contrast to the Nazi's New Order. The small minority that possesses or was arbitrarily decreed to possess a few drops of Aryan blood was, for this reason, to have the right to enslave and exploit the vast majority of those dwelling in this continent.

Fortunately the racial myth has not fallen on fertile ground in America, the land of freedom, which has always upheld as its basic principle equality of rights and opportunity for all, without distinction of origin. It is for this principle that she is now fighting against the forces of arrogance and barbarism.

I *Two Indigenous Cultures* · XII

T SEEMS TO ME ESSENTIAL, IN THE INTERESTS OF A complete understanding of the destiny of this continent, to restore to the skeptics their faith in the civilization of the leading Indian nations which dwelt here before the arrival of their Iberian conquerors. It will bolster this faith to discover that the basic human material of the Indian can be as valuable as any other in the formation of a nationality.

For this reason it seems pertinent, after having reviewed the negative forces that exist at present, to take a rapid glance at the primitive inhabitants of America and their civilization.

I shall limit myself to a brief summary of the two best-known civilizations of pre-Hispanic times: the Aztec of Mexico and the Incan of Peru.

The Indians are described by the early historians as prepossessing in their physical characteristics. Sahagún speaks of the Toltecs as being tall, so tall that they were given the name of "Tlanquacemilhuique," which means men who can run all day without resting.

The Chichimecs were strong, muscular and robust. In an account of the Acolhuas it is said of one of their armies that it was huge and powerful, and that the soldiers all looked like giants, so large were they and so "well-favored."

The picture Bernal Díaz del Castillo gives of the Emperor Montezuma in his *True Relation of the Conquest of Mexico* is a classic:

"The great Montezuma, at this time, was about forty years of age and of good stature, well-proportioned, slender and lean. His complexion was not too brown, but rather the usual color and tint of the Indian; he wore his hair not overly long, just covering his ears, with very little beard, well-arranged, thin and quite dark. His face was long, with a merry expression and gentle eyes. His bearing and his glance, in one attitude, revealed kindliness, but when necessary, gravity. He was very neat and clean in his person, bathing himself every evening. . . . He was clear of all suspicion of unnatural vices. The clothes which he wore one day he did not put on for three or four days after. He had two hundred of his nobility as a guard, in apartments adjoining his own. Of these certain people only could speak to him, and when they went to wait upon him, they had to take off their rich mantles and put on others of little value, but they had to be clean."

At the time of the Spaniards' arrival in the New World, the Aztec civilization had reached a high level in both its material and intellectual aspects. Proof is to be found in the enduring testimony left sculptured in stone as well as in the opinions of all who have studied the matter thoroughly.

The eminent historian Prescott always displayed unbounded enthusiasm for the empire of the Aztecs. In his opinion it was not only superior to any other in the New World but, by reason of its monuments, comparable to the early civilizations of Egypt and Hindustan.

The Aztecs were scrupulous in the fulfillment of their foreign obligations, and their domestic policies were characterized by a high degree of civilization. In the administration of justice, which is where the standards of a good social organization can be appreciated, they had established, as a bulwark against tyranny, a judiciary system in which the higher magistrates were independent of the king.

The religious attitude of the Aztecs can be judged by one of the prayers which Sahagún quotes in his *General History of the New Spain:* "Be patient and temperate, for God sees you and will watch over you and avenge you. Be humble toward all, and for this God will grant you mercy and honor. Neither regard with curiosity the looks or behavior of your betters, nor of women, especially married women, for the proverb says that whosoever looks with curiosity upon a woman has committed adultery with his eyes."

To be sure, the shedding of human blood in sacrifice to the gods was a blot upon this civilization. Yet even this abhorrent rite was not carried out with wanton, savage cruelty, but in a deeply religious spirit. If given his choice, the Mexican warrior would have preferred to die on the sacrificial altar rather than on the field of battle.

The domestic life and family relations of the Aztecs, on the other hand, show that they were not wanting in refinement and spiritual delicacy. Prescott describes the "fierce Aztec" with traits that are characteristic of a refined nature. They rejoiced over the good fortune of their friends and were solicitous in their hours of affliction. They were extremely polite and friendly, and showed their affection with gifts of flowers. In them was the elegant and almost ritualistic formalism of Oriental courtesy, and women were treated by their husbands in their homes with the greatest consideration and on a footing of equality.

The amazing progress of the Aztecs in astronomy, probably learned from the Mayas, is known to all, and is still testified to by the enormous block of basalt known as the Calendar of the Sun, preserved in the National Museum of Mexico. The Aztec calendar was more exact than that of Europe in the epoch of the Conquest. Although the so-called Gregorian Reform was introduced into the European calendar in 1572, the latter still remained inferior in terms of solar synchronization to that of the Aztecs of long before.

Neither were literature or poetry unknown to the primitive inhabitants of the plateau of Mexico, as can be seen from the delicate, profound poems of Netzahualcoyotl, king of Texcoco, a neighbor and ally of the Aztecs. I have not been able to resist the pleasure of quoting one of the most noteworthy of them. Its philosophic and moral tone recalls the marvelous verses of Fray Luis de León. The splendor of the lines is reminiscent of Omar Khayyam, but their philosophy is much closer to that of Ecclesiastes:

"The fading pomp of the world is like green willows, which though they aspire to endure forever are finally consumed in a sudden fire, brought down by the sharp axe, uprooted by the storm, laid low and blighted by age and decay.

"The robes of state resemble the rose in color and in fate; the beauty of the latter endures as long as its chaste buds eagerly gather and hold that part of the dawn that crystallizes in rich pearls and slowly melts into liquid dew. But as soon as the Father of living things sends down upon them the first rays of his light, he despoils them of their beauty and freshness, and that bright and purple hue they wore with such proud pleasure fades and is gone.

"All the face of the earth is a tomb. There is nothing it bears that, in the name of pity, it does not hide and bury. The rivers, the brooks, the fountains and the waters flow, and none returns to its happy source. They rush breathlessly through the vast domain of Tlaloc, and the closer they come to its far borders, the deeper they dig their melancholy tombs in which to bury themselves. What was yesterday is gone today; and today holds no promise for tomorrow.

"The sepulchers are filled with pestilent dust which was once the bones, the corpses, the bodies with souls of those who sat upon thrones, lending majesty to the canopies which covered them, presiding over assemblies, commanding armies, conquering provinces, possessing treasures, the object of devotion and reveling in their splendor, magnificence, fortune, power and admiration. These glories fade, like the terrifying smoke that is belched forth from the infernal fire of Popocatepetl, and the only monuments that recall their existence are the rough parchment on which they are written.

"Ah! Ah! What if I were to take you into the dark bosom of those sepulchers and were to ask you; which are the bones of the powerful Achalchiutlanetzin, the greatest chief of the ancient Toltecs; of Nexcamitl, the reverent worshipper of the gods? Or if I were to ask you, where is the peerless beauty of the glorious Empress Xluhtzal, and for the gentle Tlotzin, the last monarch of the unhappy Toltec kingdom? What if I were to ask you: which are the sacred ashes of our first father, Xolotl; those of the most munificent Nopal; those of the noble Tlotzin, or even for the still-warm embers of my glorious, immortal, though unhappy and ill-starred father, Ixtlixóchitl? And if I were to go on asking in this manner for all our illustrious forefathers, what would you answer? The same as I would answer: 'Indipohdi, indipohdi: I know nothing, I know nothing', because the first and the last are one with the dust. And their end shall be ours and that of those who come after us.

"Invincible princes, mighty captains, faithful friends and loyal vassals, let us aspire to, let us covet Heaven, for there all is eternal and nothing grows corrupt. The horror of the sepulcher is, for the sun, a soft cradle, and the mournful shades of darkness are, for the stars, bright lights. There is no one who has the power to dim those celestial bodies for they all serve the majestic grandeur of the Author, and they make our eyes to see now what was in the beginning and ever shall be."

That same historian of the conquest of New Spain, Bernal Díaz del Castillo, relating the visit of Cortez and some of his captains to the Great Cu, the principal temple of Tenoxtitlán, describes the capital of Mexico as a city of houses so dazzling white that, from the distance, to the covetous eyes of the conquerors they seemed to be made of silver. It had wooden drawbridges, towers and fortifications; a large, busy, crowded market place, so colorful that the Spanish soldiers who had been in Rome and in Constantinople expressed their amazement, saying that "such a well-designed and well-laid-out market place, so large and so full of people they never had seen."

The historians of this early period tell of the zoological garden that existed in the city of Mexico where live quadrupeds of every kind were to be found. Besides this, there was a Bird House filled with the most beautiful, rare and richly plumaged specimens. Another palace was a conservatory in which rare and medicinal plants were cultivated.

Molina Enríquez coincides with many other distinguished historians in calculating the pre-Spanish population of Mexico at 25,000,000 inhabitants.

Their architecture and their sculpture captivate all who visit and study their majestic ruins. The delicacy of their pottery can be compared with that of the classic relics of the old civilizations. They had discovered bronze and worked in gold, silver and copper.

The French writer, Paul Morand, has this to say: "These hard, realistic men of the Aztec and pre-Aztec days were prodigious sculptors. In the epoch of the Mayas they were more graceful and decorative. The simplification of planes and volumes, the very things our moderns are trying to do, was discovered by them at one stroke. . . . In the field of pure statuary, such works as the 'Head of a Dead Man', in basalt, of the pre-Aztec period, or the 'Head of the Eagle Knight' are of such strength that Rodin, I have been told, was roused to admiration."

The information we possess concerning the physical characteristics of the Incas indicates that, like the Indians of Mexico, the inhabitants of Peru, at the time of the conquest, were a race full of vigor.

Atahualpa, the emperor of the Incas, with whom Francisco Pizarro first had contact, is described by Prescott as a strong, well-built man, with a broad head and a face that would have been handsome had it not been that his blood-shot eyes gave his physiognomy a cruel expression.

The same American historian, referring to one of the Inca captains whom the Spaniards had to fight when they besieged certain strongholds, describes him in Homeric terms, as a man of athletic build, armed with shield and breast plate, who patrolled the battlements brandishing a huge war club studded with copper points. This Indian Hercules, with his formidable weapon, dashed into the abyss the Spaniards who attempted to scale the walls.

Although the civilization of the Incas differed greatly in many aspects from that of the Aztecs, being superior in some and inferior in others, in general the two were analagous in the degree of their development.

The whole social organization was based on a wisely conceived plan. One is struck by the great number of their laws and decrees against idleness and poverty.

The religion of the Incas, as compared with that of the Aztecs, was on a higher spiritual plane in both its concepts and its rites. Human sacrifices were unknown; the Incas believed in the resurrection; and good and evil were duly rewarded in the other life.

The wealth of the Peruvian nobles and of the Incan Empire was really extraordinary. The Inca Garcilaso relates that in the palace of one of the Incan princes, the blankets and bed-covers of vicuna wool were so fine and delicate that they were sent to King Philip II "as objects that are greatly esteemed in those lands." The main square of Cuzco is described by the historian Sarmiento, about the middle of the XVIth century, as being far superior to those of Jerusalem, Rome and Persia in its abundance of gold, silver, gems and every form of wealth.

Yet it was probably in their control of the forces of nature and their development of their agricultural resources, as well as in the field of architecture, that the Incas displayed their greatest inventive and creative powers.

At times their ruins surpass those of the ancient Romans in grandeur, and there is a great resemblance between the material civilizations of the two, in their aqueducts, their walls, their military highways and their fortresses. The remains of these that can still be seen and the terraced mountainsides reveal a scientific knowledge that astounds the most modern engineers of our own day.

To sum up these two great civilizations, the Incan and the Aztec, I could not do better than quote these words of tribute to the native race by Dr. Manuel Gamio:

"It was the American Indian who, many centuries before the Conquest, experimented with, selected, cultivated and made use of countless plants which were unknown before. As proof of the value of the Indians' contribution to Europe, there is this list of valuable animal and vegetable products compiled by diligent scholars in the field: corn, potato, sweet potato, tomato, different kinds of chile, large and small squash, several varieties of beans, black pepper, pineapple, medlar, Barbadoes cherry, persimmon, papaya, guava, peanut, oca, walnut, haw, Capulin cherry, maté tea, alligator pear, custard apple, tobacco, quinine, buckthorn bark, coca, Kola (mallow), sisal, rubber, copal, balsam of Peru, indigo, cochineal, logwood, axe for lacquers, and many others we cannot recall at the moment. As for animals: alpaca, llama, vicuna, bison, Guinea pig, Mexican dog, chinchilla, musk-duck, turkey, etc.

"Who found and developed the deposits of placer gold, the metal which was the magnet of the Conquest? Who discovered, experimented with and made use of the building materials which the Spaniards adopted and which are extensively used today? Who built the enduring, sumptuous architectural monuments of Tlahuanaco, Pachacamac, Chichen Itza, Mitla, Teotihuacán, and the pueblos of Arizona and New Mexico? Who worked out calendars that measured time more exactly than the Gregorian or the Julian? Who wove the marvelous fabrics of Peru, who wrought the embossed and filigree work in gold and copper of Panama, Ecuador, Colombia, Peru and Mexico which the goldsmiths of Renaissance Italy and Spain gazed on with admiration and amazement? All this was the work of the Indian who, from the prehistoric days of his arrival on this continent labored untiringly to make himself master of the American world and enjoy its rich products."

The native races of Latin America reached a high degree of civilization and their material achievements in many fields of human endeavor were stupendous. But this does not mean in any sense that it is possible to revive these vanished civilizations or that it should be attempted. The days of Montezuma and the plumed serpent, whose return D. H. Lawrence dreamed of, are gone forever.

Exaggeration is always a dangerous thing. The splendor of those ancient Indian civilizations is valuable to refute those who argue that the Indian is of no value as basic human material; but it should not blind us to the very evident decadence, both cultural and biological, into which they have fallen, from a variety of causes quite well known. And still less should it lead us to infer that only the aboriginal race can serve as a basis for the future population of the whole continent. No, what we should try to create is a higher type of American civilization into which the Indian can be gradually incorporated by means of eugenic racial cross-breeding which, unfortunately, could not be carried out during the Conquest, nor has it been given any thought since our independence. The result of this would, in time, be a homogeneous New World.

It can be categorically stated that the Latin-American of the future will not be white, but neither will he be Indian; he will be a blend: the *mestizo*. History has proved that cross-breeding, far from being a source of inferiority, has been a magnificent fountain of strength. In the most civilized nations of Europe, their hour of greatest splendor has always coincided with the moment of maximum racial mixing. Neither Greece, in the time of Pericles, nor Italy in the days of Michael Angelo, nor France under Louis XIV, were ethnically pure.

To bring about the formation of this homogeneous population will be a tremendous task. But an intelligently directed civilization, with great waves of immigration and emigration, with economic, social and cultural progress, will provide America with the genuine American type, cleansed of vices and invigorated with the good qualities of each race. America should prepare to receive the eager tide of European races waiting to emigrate. Along with the work of receiving this influx of new population and fusing its various ethnological groups, must go the equally necessary task of steadfastly and conscientiously improving the biological quality of the American.

The changing of the present deficient diet of the mass of Latin-Americans; the development of public hygiene and the improvement of sanitary conditions; the campaign against alcoholism and against endemic and epidemic diseases of the different countries, and the organized and systematic propagation of eugenics, are other measures which should be put into practice to bring about the biological liberation of the Americas.

So vast and arduous a task calls for both private and state

initiative. But if the plan is to be decisively pushed, there must be inter-American action.

Fortunately the efforts already made in this direction have been of such undeniable importance that even the most skeptical cannot fail to grasp their implication for the future. This effort alone would be sufficient to confirm our faith in the incalculable scope and advantages inherent in the union of America.

The Eighth Inter-American Conference held in Lima in 1938 pointed out the importance of demography in the Americas and adopted resolutions bearing upon immigration to the end that there should be no distinctions of race, class or creed. Standard treaties were proposed to guide and direct effectively and adequately the flow of immigration to America. These took into account the need of plans for financial co-operation to assist this immigration.

In this way, special recognition is given to the need for new blood to strengthen the races of this continent, particularly in the countries of Latin America. Although the war has interrupted for the time being inter-American activities in this field, there is no doubt that, once peace is restored, they will again become the concern of all the states in the New World.

The Congress of Pátzcuaro gave special attention to the biological problem, devoting all the studies of its first session to this question. A number of resolutions and recommendations were adopted with the object of improving living conditions among the native population, and combating the principal diseases from which they suffer.

This generous movement for the biological improvement of the American stock shows how far we are, in the ideals which inspire the union of the nations of America, from Hitler's racial doctrines. America upholds the just principle of equality of rights and opportunity for all human beings, regardless of race or origin.

THE COUNTRIES OF THIS CONTINENT HAVE BEEN variously endowed by nature. Some, because of their relatively small area or their lack of natural wealth, are able to supply only a small part of their needs, while others have a great variety and abundance of products. Yet even the United States, Brazil and Mexico, which are blessed with vast potential resources, are far from producing all that they require. Therefore, like the rest of the world, the nations of America must depend, to a greater or lesser degree, and especially in times of war, on other countries.

This interdependence grows greater every day, despite the increase in production and the discovery of new substitutes, because of the ever-growing demands of modern life. To bring these raw materials from other continents means, with rare exceptions, increased costs, transportation difficulties, delay and, in time of war, enormous risks, irreplaceable losses and, often, the impossibility of obtaining supplies. This war drives the gravity of the problem home to us every day.

The obvious solution for the nations of America is to try to obtain needed manufactured products, especially the raw materials, within the continent itself. That is tantamount to saying that an economic policy of unity must be worked out which will foster agriculture, stock-raising, mining, and the harnessing of sources of power and industrialization.

Frequently Pan Americanism is examined with skepticism on the ground that our economies are antagonistic. The natural market of one or another region, it is said, is unsatisfactory for the exchange of products because neither is a reciprocal consumer, and both are obliged to sell to the same buyer, *viz* Europe, because of rival rather than collaborating interests.

All this represents the dead weight of the past, but is far from the growing possibilities the future holds. The American continent offers a geographical and spiritual unity so unique that its economic organization should constitute a natural and spontaneous bloc, a co-operative unit within the rest of world economy.

It goes without saying that the exchange of goods should tend to utilize every possibility of mutual consumption. At present the economy of the Americas is improperly organized. The United States and Argentina, with similar climates because of their similar situations on opposite extremes of the globe, turn out the same products and instead of being able to exchange them are forced into self-interested competition. Wheat, barley, hides, meat, corn, must necessarily take the European route because the United States produces an excess and the other American countries lack consumption power.

The production of other American countries, especially those facing the Pacific, has been forgotten in world economy; they lack communications and the active commercial interchange to which they might aspire.

Obviously, therefore, all that is lacking is organization to create a market that would expand with increasing rapidity along with the economic expansion of our countries.

The tropical countries will be logical and large consumers of wheat, refrigerated and tinned meats, and hides, in exchange for their varied products—now potential—of fibers, rubber, tropical fruits, once their economy is developed and the urgently needed communications are established, elements without which our economic unity cannot be maintained.

This does not signify the inauguration of a closed continental autarchy. But the world, in its economic organization, will endeavor to follow the logical and natural line offering the largest number of communication facilities and in accordance with geographical affinity. This tendency, which has the force of natural law, is what will give the form of continental blocs to the plans for world co-ordination in the future. In the Americas this co-ordination of our countries has a superior strength, for it is already molded to realities, with extraordinary practical, ideological and spiritual possibilities. It should not be forgotten, however, that such continental organizations should be made to serve better the higher purposes of world solidarity.

In the present conflict, the peoples of the continent are making the geographical contribution of their air and naval bases and the patrolling of their coasts and territory. At the same time they are producing to the limits of their capacity, not only war materials, but all kinds of products required for the maintenance of the armies in the field and the civilian populations of their allies.

Yet despite the whole-hearted co-operation of all the peoples of America, the effects of the disunion, poverty and lack of preparation in which we have lived are making themselves felt. If all our nations had been able to utilize their vast resources, and, in unity and friendly understanding, had been able to develop in peace time their production and prepare for war, what an immense contribution they would now be rendering in these tragic hours when the liberty, integrity and sovereignty of a continent are at stake! An international organization, based on confidence and friendship and resting on law, was lacking; but now that the bases for this are being laid, the time is at hand to co-ordinate our economic resources and set up a unified economy for all the American nations.

If the events of the present war cannot be foreseen, even less is it possible to envision the alternatives of peace. But in any case, what can be affirmed is that the establishment of permanent peace will be the most transcendental objective of the post-war period. This objective cannot be attained without the delegation of a minimum of sovereignty indispensable for the creation of an international organization that will settle disputes and utilize the means to enforce its decisions.

We can affirm that universal sentiment dictates an end of wars; but recognizing man's nature, we must conclude that in a world which daily invents such great destructive powers, the only way to maintain the peace is to be in a position to defend it against unexpected aggressions.

The triumph of those who seek war must be made impossible, and this can be realized by uniting all peoples on the basis of social justice and well-being, putting them in a condition to overpower those who, in a given moment, might yield to the barbaric temptation of war.

This does not signify an armament race. It means only that pacific peoples should have the necessary means of defense. Among these defenses, above all, they should be able to count on the necessary raw materials so they can meet the exigencies of a state of war.

Even in the calmest moments in the life of nations and even after the most efficient international agencies for world peace have been established, until there exists a minimum of international law properly upheld by international tribunals with armed forces at their disposition, provision must be made for all the necessary civil and military resources, even for a blockade, to insure against the eventuality of war, and foster the constructive efforts of peace. The day will come when some organization of nations will guarantee security forever. But in the meantime, peace itself will call for war-preparedness. To neglect this would leave the world at the mercy of swift unexpected assaults.

Nothing would so eloquently and clearly demonstrate the advantage of the system alluded to for the integrated defense of this hemisphere, during war and during peace, as would a study of the principal strategic materials obtainable on this continent.

The term "strategic materials" applied to raw materials does not exactly correspond with reality for, as has been indicated, in times of war and in intimate relation to war, all raw materials are necessary, be they destined to civil or to military uses, if a country at war is to develop all its combative power.

The leading Powers have lists of strategic materials, lists which have to be modified constantly, to a greater or lesser degree, to keep them abreast of the changing circumstances peculiar to each nation. For example, the government of the United States has been making a careful study of its needs with reference to its particular situation, and as a result has drawn up a list of essential leading products, which already has undergone some slight modification. In this list, besides power, which is not strictly speaking a prime material, it includes foodstuffs, iron and steel, machinery, chemicals and medicines, coal, iron ore, petroleum and derivatives, copper, lead, nitrates, sulphur and pyrites, cotton, aluminum, zinc, rubber, manganese, nickel, chromium, tungsten, wool, potassium, phosphates, antimony, tin, mercury and mica.

To be sure, these twenty-six products or groups of products are not the only ones to which the term "strategic" should be applied, but only the most important of them, or the most difficult to obtain or substitute. At present the United States is the richest country in raw materials in the world and, for this reason, the one which closest approaches autarchy. Nevertheless, it is far from achieving it for, of some of these materials, which its government considers essential, it has only a small part of what is needed.

The essential industrial products and critical raw materials that the United States has at its disposal fall into four groups:

First, materials which it produces in quantities greater than, equal to, or slightly below its needs: foodstuffs, iron, steel, machinery, chemicals and medicines, coal, iron ore, petroleum and its derivatives, lead, sulphur, cotton, zinc and phosphates.

Second, products whose scarcity would be felt, since only fifty per cent of the amount required is available, such as nitrates, aluminum and wool.

Third, products of which the United States produces only about a third of what it needs: tungsten, potassium, mercury and mica.

Fourth, raw materials whose shortage would be serious, if they could not be brought in from abroad, since the national production is able to supply only ten per cent or less of its needs: rubber, manganese, nickel, chromium, antimony and tin (the tin produced in United States territory is only three per cent of what that country needs in case of war).

As can be seen, modern metallurgy, which is the corner-stone of contemporary civilization, is one of most eloquent proofs of the interdependence of the world. This civilization depends on a series of metals which are of value only when combined and which are useless by themselves. Iron, however abundant, does not attain its maximum value unless mixed with chromium or manganese. This explains why the war has been termed a race for strategic materials. We could put it this way: Pan Americanism has a metallic skeleton. By this I mean that just because this civilization, chiefly metallurgical, requires the alliance of all our countries so as to make available the products of its mines, its metallurgical resources, and so as to supply those strategic materials which were previously brought from the four corners of the earth, the unity of our continent, from this aspect, enters the category of an absolute necessity if its greatness and safety are to be maintained.

In the eighteen million square miles of this American continent, we must manage to find quickly the vital materials which the war has made it impossible to bring from other lands to supply the missing links of the metallurgical chain. We can understand the United States' pressing need to find substitutes for metals such as tin, chromium and manganese, for without them unquestionably the whole armament and defense program would have been hampered, endangering the final outcome of this world conflict.

It is impressive to see how the United States, without regard for the standard of living which will be markedly reduced, is imposing rapid and drastic measures to insure the necessary supply of metals for military requirements. To this end it has prohibited the manufacture for non-military use of products which use the following metals: manganese, chromium, mercury, tungsten, nickel, tin, antimony, copper, zinc, lead, aluminum and magnesium. Who knows when these metals again will be available for civilian use? Only the end of the war will give the answer.

The intensive production of all these metals is stupendous. Only tin seems an insoluble problem, for even if the mines of all America are worked to capacity, they cannot supply that which has been cut off from sources no longer available to the United States.

The Bureau of Mines of the United States has sent its best experts over the whole continent in search of ore deposits. Each one of these metals has acquired a tremendous and hitherto-unsuspected importance, and the great scarcity of some of them is now being felt. At the same time, the mere thought of their being exploited in an unbridled fashion arouses great concern, for certain of them, aluminum for example (which has been called the basic metal of present-day civilization) will, if all the reserves in the United States are fully exploited, be totally exhausted in six years. The same is true of oil deposits.

War is a frightful glutton for metals; it devours the bowels of the earth. Chemistry has come to the aid of metallurgy, making and extracting products from the most ordinary materials, as for example, aluminum from clay (bauxite), or, still more extraordinary, magnesium from sea water. Nevertheless, the most important metallurgical resources are disappearing even in nations like the United States, whose supplies were considered inexhaustible.

Our present civilization is based on metals scattered capriciously over the face of the globe. When we realize that on this American continent we have been so blessed that by pooling our resources we can supply nearly all our needs for strategic materials, then is strengthened our conviction of the privilege that continental union represents.

A Economic Solidarity & Social Justice · XIV

ALL NATIONS SHOULD HAVE EQUAL ACCESS TO markets of basic raw materials, as the Atlantic Charter proclaims, but they should also have this same access to manufactured products. Inequality of such opportunity sets up preferential conditions directly affecting the standard of living of the different countries. This false equation—a relic of colonial days—by which lands that sell their raw materials at starvation prices are obliged to buy manufactured goods at exorbitant rates, must be done away with. Equality of purchase price for industrial products is one of the formulas for economic equality in opportunities for social well-being.

These ends can be achieved only by developing the purchasing power of the different countries through decent wages and widespread opportunity for work. But since this alone would not suffice if imported products are priced beyond the consumers' means, it will likewise be absolutely necessary to eliminate all the unjustifiable motives for elevating prices, such as needless middlemen, excessive freight-rates, prohibitive tariffs; and, whenever raw materials can be processed to advantage in the country of origin, this should be done to promote industrialization.

As far as national markets are concerned, the state already takes it upon itself to guarantee, as far as possible, conditions of free competition. Within every nation exist measures especially designed to restrain unfair practices springing from artificial control of production, trusts, cartels and international syndicates, all of which interfere with the free play of supply and demand and tend to fix prices on the basis of private monopoly.

At the same time the state prohibits differential transportation rates, or sanctions them only to re-establish the equality disturbed by unequal conditions. And finally, it abolishes internal customs barriers.

All this means that in the national markets there exists a system of controls previously set up which functions throughout the economic process. This implies a degree of intervention on the part of the state in the fixing of prices. Moreover—and this is important—since within the same country there is a certain uniformity in wages because of the similarity in the mode of living among workers of the same class, the costs of production must be in keeping.

The situation in international markets is very different. There are no safeguards or regulations or state vigilance against unfair competitive practices. As a result, the final exchange is wholly *laissez faire,* so that the prices in vogue merely seem to correspond to the conditions of a free market. Actually supply is often controlled at its source by private international organizations whose operations at times extend to all the countries in which production of a given type is possible. For this reason, prices are fixed in these markets by the arbitrary decision of powerfully organized producers. In international commerce there are more than forty mineral and agricultural products subject to the arbitrary control of consortiums and private corporations.

Now let us see what happens to products not thus controlled which innocently and guilelessly appear upon the international markets. If they are left to the mercy of cutthroat competition, there ensues a grossly unfair struggle between these unprotected, scattered products and the organized merchandise bloc, that results in the unjust sacrifice of the defenseless producers.

Without attempting to make an iron-clad generalization, it may be said that the articles not controlled are the basic agricultural products, and those under control are elaborated food products and manufactures.

This explains, to a large extent, the great difference in economic level of countries belonging to one category or the other. And if to this unfavorable and unequal situation between the countries producing raw materials and the industrialized countries, we add the fact that in the latter the use of machinery gives an extraordinary superiority to their organization and control, it is easy to understand the discouragement of the agricultural nations confronted with the favored situation of the industrialized nations.

Agricultural production, because of the conditions attendant upon plant growth and the caprices of weather to which crops are subjected before coming to maturity, is beset by risks, hazards and limitations. On the other hand, the use of the machine makes for precision, flexibility and an almost total mastery of production. The returns from agriculture are uncertain and do not give a firm basis for credit. By contrast, industrial profits, being more stable, can be calculated beforehand, for purposes of insurance and credit. Industry is concentration; agriculture, dispersion. Therefore industrial production lends itself easily to the formation of combines, international cartels, trusts, or "gentlemen's agreements."

Here we find the explanation for the tragedy of the low level of farm wages in Latin America, a condition which reacts on the economy of the whole continent and is aggravated by the fact that the Latin-American worker must shoulder another burden, that of the high cost of manufactured goods.

By the time imported manufactures reach the humble American consumer, after the costs of customs duties, middlemen, transportation and domestic taxes have been added, they are beyond his reach. This bars him from the benefits of civilization.

The lack of stability and the inequality which envelop agricultural life confronted with industrial life, carry over into the international sphere by setting the agricultural nations against the industrialized nations. In domestic economy the field is in contraposition to the factory; in labor union activity, the farm workers against organized workers. In all these concentric spheres, the same inequality affects all those engaged in agriculture—agricultural nations and farm owners and farmworkers. Each group is lacerated by inferiority to the factors of industry—industrialized nations, corporations or industrial entrepreneurs, and unionized workers—whose conditions, compared to the former, constitute real privileges. A sentiment of equality should diminish the crudity of these inequalities, among nations as well as among individuals.

Many of the fruitful experiences of the New Deal to aid the farmer, redeeming him from the unjust inequality to which the blind economic forces have condemned him, indicate the appropriate course, not only for the domestic life of the United States but also for the international life of the Americas. Crop insurance, the ever-normal granary plan, the deposit warehouses and export subsidies, constitute a fertile experimental field for discovering the correct solution.

Limiting ourselves to the international scene, we believe that if there is to be a strong effort to rectify this inequality in order to benefit all and restore confidence to those countries depending primarily on agriculture, there could be no method more just than that of destroying the evils of the dispersion of farming by giving it cohesion and weapons of defense, at the same time making manufactured products accessible to the peoples of America by augmenting their purchasing power and preventing unwarranted price jumps.

The problem is further complicated by the striking difference between industrial and farm wages. Substantial differences exist, it is true, between the wages paid in similar industries in the United States and Latin America; but the differences in agricultural wages are really deplorable. For example, in 1937 the average wage paid to workers in the oil fields in the United States was about $8 a day, while in Mexico the average per eight-hour day was 7 Mexican pesos. Although the Mexican worker received only 15 per cent of the pay earned by the North American, this was compensated for to a considerable degree by the difference in the cost of living of the two countries.

Agricultural wage differences and inequalities are much greater. In Honduras, the average wage can be calculated at about $20 a month; in Brazil, from $15 to $20; in Mexico, from $4 to $10; and in certain countries of Central America, Colombia, Ecuador and Bolivia, from $4 to $8; whereas in the United States on the average, the farm laborer, in some years, has made as much as $50 a month or more.

Without taking into consideration grains, vegetables, and other products consumed locally, whose production costs and wages are calculated by national averages, bananas, coffee, rubber and hemp are four examples of the unfair system of production in our agricultural countries. The solution to the problems they involve must be continent-wide.

The value of the banana per large bunch in the United States—the chief importer—is $4.30, whereas the cost of production in Mexico is not more than 25 cents, Mexican money, for cultivation costs and 20 cents for profit and handling. Therefore the banana-raising regions have received in wages only 10 cents of the $4.30 the bunch brings. The huge difference is not due to other expenses nor does it represent the grower's profit. It is distributed almost wholly among the shipping companies, jobbers and middlemen who come between the producer and the consumer. The nature of the fruit is such—it demands comparatively rapid transportation under refrigeration—that certain shipping companies have set up what amounts to a monopoly of it. The solution would seem to be to make available to the banana-raising countries the necessary means of transportation and set up a great Pan-American Mercantile Exchange which would eliminate the middleman and bring the producers into direct relation with the consumers of the whole continent.

At the same time, the Exchange, in its capacity as clearing house, would carry out all transactions, transfers, settlements and such other banking operations as fall within the province of an agency of this type. In this way, besides eliminating countless abuses of other sorts, the greater part of the price of the fruit would go to the plantation owners and workers, raising their returns by about 200 per cent. This same procedure could be adopted for all tropical fruits and articles of international trade that require rapid and efficient transportation. The abolishment of the imperialism exercised by the great fruit transportation companies would represent a great step in the economic progress of the Continent.

Rubber presents a different problem. Its present price of 22 cents a pound, due to the war, cannot be maintained once peace is restored, and it probably will drop to 9 cents a pound, its price a few years ago, unless preventive measures are taken. Until now the price of this product has been so low, because of the competition of markets of the Far East, that any increase in wages would have affected its sale price prohibitively.

The price of natural rubber should be in keeping with that of the synthetic variety since, although it is inferior to the latter in certain aspects, it is far superior in others. This artificial rubber brings around 50 cents a pound. The trouble lies in the fact that the rubber of America, which constitutes only about three per cent of the world output, has to compete in peace time with that of Asia and the East Indies, where wages are at starvation levels. In India, Borneo, the Dutch East Indies, Indo-China, rubber is raised on huge plantations under a system of imperialist domination of colonial type, and its price is determined there.

In Latin America the production of rubber has not been developed as it should precisely because the great international trusts have preferred to make enormous investments in those distant quarters of the globe where low wages are the basis of huge profits. To compete in their small-scale production, which depends solely upon wild rubber, the Latin American countries have had to adapt wages and labor conditions to this same colonial system of exploitation. For rubber, just as for other products of a similar nature—copra, quinine, palm, fibers and oil-bearing seeds—it will be necessary to establish some form of protection against the competition of slave wages unless the world can work out an interdependent system of world economy.

To put this transcendental problem of assuring wages compatible with human dignity—as is demanded by the principles of human solidarity for which we are fighting—and especially because of its major importance for the poorer countries of the world whose fate should be our special concern, I would venture the following suggestion: the creation of a permanent international institute, with authority to impose general standards of action which all states would have to accept as a preliminary condition to the right to participate in international commerce.

Many and diverse matters would have to be studied and taken into consideration by such an institute. It would have to assemble a large and competent personnel in the world's most important production centers. Its primary mission would be to gather detailed information regarding production conditions, costs, salaries, taxes, shipping tariffs by land, sea and river, legal restrictions, harbor, docking and lighterage charges; in a word, all the costs that in one way or another affect the conditions of free production and, as a consequence, fair competition in world markets.

One matter which should receive special attention from this institute is that of production, carried on in countries where wages are so low as to make for ruinous competition and are contrary to human freedom, in order that international trading in such materials be forbidden until rectification of the social outrage of compensation unworthy of the new civilization toward which the world is working.

All over the globe people are eager to establish world cooperation and break down the walls behind which rabid nationalisms fortify themselves. However, we must guard against a lack of realism that would lead to confusion. The final goal is a world-wide economic order in which wages and prices —with proper consideration for local conditions—would be equalized everywhere. By close watch upon the different factors of consumption and production, economic activities could be regulated so as to eliminate to a great extent all inequalities and to guarantee, under an economy of plenty, a fair distribution of wealth and enduring solidarity among the peoples of the earth. The ultimate outcome of all these activities would be the lessening of all risks for the leading products, especially agricultural, which enter into international commerce. The progress realized by meteorology and the great increase in the number of weather bureaus make it possible to establish with sufficient reliability the correct time and conditions for bringing in crops; also, on the basis of consumption data, the requisite amount of any given metal can be predetermined. For all such raw materials it is possible, by perfecting statistical methods and widening their application, to establish adequate flexible quotas. There is no longer any reason why human intelligence should not step in to save men and nations from blind competition, which brings such unnecessary ruin and misery.

But in view of the vastness of the enterprise, we cannot hope to see it carried to fruition in one move, nor can we act as if the goal we aspire to were already achieved.

It seems to me that it would be a sound procedure—while the path of an international, universal economy is being patiently hewed out—for America, to guarantee a certain economic security and an adequate standard of living, to establish a decent wage level and a distribution of production that will free her peoples from the constant threat of periodic crises of unemployment and poverty. It would constitute a basis for inter-American solidarity if we could arrange an interchange of our products and our standards of social justice so well planned there would be no danger in adhering to it—before we ventured, without sufficient guarantee, upon a project for world economy lacking the requisite controls. We will have to recognize that there exists an urgent need for America to honor her obligation to redeem her masses by establishing a high standard of living and that we will have to resort to defensive measures, as indicated, to uphold continental principles, so that, at least in America, the doors would be closed to merchandise tainted with the stigma of labor unjustly remunerated. At the same time, we must establish our economic unit and make absolutely firm our great spiritual gains.

Here we can point out one of the simplest ways in which the United States government has been encouraging the production of certain of the agricultural products we have been speaking of, such as quinine and rubber. As large investments are required and many years must elapse before production yields returns, it has drawn up long-term contracts with certain companies for their output. This economic policy is undoubtedly safer than large investments in distant continents, as the war has proved all too convincingly.

But the final and obvious solution will be to so arrange the economic map of the Americas as to guarantee stabilized production and planned distribution, thus assuring the economic security of each of our countries. This will give the additional benefit that the production of prime materials of a strategic nature, such as rubber, oil and defense minerals, which should constitute the common property of the continent, can be controlled in an ordered manner and reserves maintained as dictated by foresight and experience.

I am sure that sooner or later these policies will be put into practice throughout the world, but in the meantime this hemisphere should, in one of its assemblies, study the best way to create an institute with sufficient powers to control and organize our economy. The true solidarity of the American nations should manifest itself in both war and peace, something that will be achieved by replacing the anarchy in which they have lived with economic and strategical unification.

With regard to coffee, the average price of fifteen cents a pound leaves ample margin for increasing the wages of the workers, who now receive only one or two cents of this price. For both coffee and cocoa, which fall in the same category, much of what has been said of bananas and rubber holds true, but there also exists another factor, unique and of great importance, which is that our continent produces 50 per cent of the world's supply. The rest is divided among Asia, 35 per cent; Africa, 14 per cent; and Oceania, one per cent. Therefore these products are not wholly consumed in America, as is the rubber grown on this continent, but must be exported to Europe. As a result, continental protection would not be enough, and some plan of price fixing for export would have to be worked out. There would have to be one price for inter-American commerce so that it would not be affected by the competition of similar products from countries exploited under a colonial system. Then, for sales outside the continent, the price would have to be such as to meet competition, with export quotas for each producing country. The losses on export sales would be spread by a "Commission for Price-Fixing and Exportation" in such a way as to be taken up insensibly by all the producers of the continent.

Sisal (henequen) represents a more complicated problem as its price is affected to a certain degree by the price of Manila hemp, which is of better quality, as well as by the interests of the North American companies that manufacture binder twine, the principal use of sisal hemp. Until 1915, Manila hemp brought nine cents a pound while sisal stayed at about seven cents. But from then on, while the price of the former rose quickly to more than 16 cents a pound—even poorer grades not so good as sisal—the latter was artificially pegged at 7½ cents. A Commission for Controlling the Henequen Market was set up in México to look after the price of the Mexican product, and in 1918 it was able to bring the price up to 19¼ cents a pound.

Nevertheless, after World War I, it finally lost the heroic fight it had put up against the North American trusts. The result was a terrific crisis when the bottom dropped out of the market and the price fell to 10½ cents a pound. Not even at this figure could the Commission dispose of the enormous stocks on hand, nor even of the annual production. When the Commission went out of existence, the buyers forced the price down still further, to 3¼ cents a pound, bringing about the complete ruination of Yucatán.

In 1941 the price of sisal was 5¼ cents a pound, and at present, by the terms of a special agreement with the United States, it has gone up to 9 cents, a figure that scarcely makes possible wages of 50 cents a day, and this only because the dollar is worth 4.85 Mexican pesos. In view of the great rise in the cost of living, this wage is completely inadequate.

The only solution to the sisal problem would be local industrialization. But to do this, since Yucatán does not have sufficient capital to build the plants that would be needed, a generous gesture would have to be made to finance and organize the enterprise and supply the machinery.

As with henequen, so with a multitude of Latin American products, the wages of the producers can be raised only if the materials are processed at the point of origin, thus avoiding transportation charges, losses, competition with distant sources of supply and arbitrary and artificial price-fixing. The foregoing involves a new economic policy, which, in reason and justice, would plan the industrialization of the Continent.

It is absolutely indispensable in exploiting raw materials to install plants where production is easiest and most convenient for creating the industrial specialization of each region of

America, in effect a chain of subsidiary plants distributed throughout the continent to manufacture the same articles. In this way, in each region, the cost of raw materials and wages would have a proper ratio to that of the finished articles, which could then be sold everywhere at more or less the same price.

It is pertinent to point out here that the extraction of non-precious minerals and other sub-soil products has many features in common with those we have referred to in agriculture. Mining also involves much risk and, moreover, is subordinated to the smelting industries to which it supplies the raw materials. Each manufactured product requires steel, iron, copper, metalloids, etc., of different characteristics and specifications, which makes the process of recovery and refining of the minerals of greatest importance and requires complicated, expensive, large-scale plants. These smelting companies or the industrial consortiums which use these minerals as their raw materials, fix the prices to suit themselves. The countries which have to export their minerals as ore or, at best, as concentrates, are in the same situation, as regards the mining industry, as those typically agricultural.

An idea frequently encountered is that a new industry will compete with similar ones in other countries, to the economic detriment of the latter. As a salutary example, let us consider the United States and Canada. The reciprocally beneficial trade has been in no way harmed by the fact that Canada has achieved a high degree of industrialization. On the contrary, the economy of both has been strengthened.

Industrial planning for America would have to be done with a thorough knowledge of the physical, human and economic possibilities of each region and of the hemisphere as a whole. Planning of this sort would rule out the establishment of industries that were predestined from the start to ruin and failure. When a factory is set up in a place that is difficult to reach, or far away from production centers of raw materials, or sources of power, or where the climate is bad or labor scarce or unsatisfactory, its products, because of their high costs or inferior quality, cannot meet competition and the enterprise fails, with lamentable loss of effort and capital; or else it has to be artificially protected by the state, by means of tariffs, and the consumer is the victim because of the increased cost. This deplorable situation is wholly unnecessary because there is not a single region in America which could not develop the industries appropriate to its natural and human resources.

Therefore the need of rational planning is imposed by natural circumstances. As an example, let us take the United States, because of the extent of its territory and the variety of its raw materials. It is not by chance that its great industries are concentrated in the Northeast, close to the coal and iron mines and the hydroelectric plants of Niagara. The motion picture industry follows the sun and scenery of California. The textile industries have sought the damp climates which lessen the danger of breaking threads and the consequent stoppage of the looms. Chicago, that railroad center to which livestock can so easily be shipped, is the stockyard and meat-packing hub. Oil refineries, flour mills and canning factories, on the other hand, are scattered all over the country wherever the raw materials are found.

In the same way, all over America, packing houses, canning factories for fruit and tropical products, and smelters should be set up wherever convenient, while textile mills, foundries, blast furnaces and machine works should be concentrated in a few places. Chemical dye plants, precision lens and other highly specialized industries could be limited to one or two places in the hemisphere.

The setting up of industries in lands hitherto given over to agriculture and raw material production would, by thus processing the goods within the country, permit the lowest cost and make them accessible to popular consumption, thus raising the standard of living. In this way, the acquisitive capacity of many groups, till now unable to buy, would open up new markets for much larger quantities of articles, not only those of the developing new industries in each country, but also those of nations already industrialized, for the needs and the consuming capacity of each country would be progressively augmented. If the relative cost of production increased because the producers of raw materials received better prices for their goods, the manufacturers would be compensated by the greater volume of sales. Naturally, the degree of basic industrialization it is wise to introduce into the agricultural countries must be taken into consideration. The ideal would be gradually to leave more and more to the highly industrialized countries the manufacture of those articles which—either because they require large capital investments or need world markets to make them profitable and therefore require special conditions of location, sources of power, and specialized techniques—are not suited for local production in each country.

The fertility of the land, no matter how flourishing the agriculture it supports, is but one step in the creation of a complete civilization. The development of industry and manufactures is absolutely necessary to consolidate the real economic strength of a nation. The farm, even in the most privileged agricultural countries, is unable to absorb the whole working population. The excess of farm workers needs to be absorbed by industries. Without this opportunity it is impossible for a people to escape misery. Only when agriculture and manufacturing complement each other does the financial life of a country become a complete circulatory system; otherwise the wealth of a country bleeds away as in a broken vein, for the returns of agriculture are drawn off to strengthen the industries of other lands, and the nation loses all possibilities of economic expansion.

All these plans, which offer no problems to modern technology, cannot succeed without ample credits, boldly distributed.

When one attempts to understand what at first glance seems a mystery—Germany's ability to build an economy which could forge the immense equipment of war she has been using in this struggle—one needs only to observe the credit miracles of that country.

That economic genius, Hjalmar Schacht, saw that every man in Germany had to be put to work. But this was not possible unless into the hands of each was put the credit needed to turn him into a producing element.

If, as a famous thinker has said, it is a proof of intelligence to imitate the good qualities of an enemy, America should hasten to give every one of her men who has the capacity and preparation the necessary credits to contribute to the coming greatness of this continent.

The field for investments is unlimited for various generations. The conquest of nature over an expanse of forty million square kilometers will absorb all our constructive capacity for the present. After the war, roads, airports, air lines, the construction of millions of homes for American workers, the sanitation of our cities, urbanization, agricultural development of the richest regions of the world, the building of ships and shipyards, the exploitation of hydraulic resources, and, together with these great undertakings, the work of the factories which are to turn out the machinery and the products needed for this vast reconstruction plan, will revolutionize the world and establish in America the permanent bases of its economic greatness, its liberty and its imperishable union.

Financing of the agricultural nations will require medium and long-term credits, and for the best results they should be extended after a thorough technical study of the condition of the agricultural enterprises to be aided, and a careful watch kept on the manner in which they are used.

Obviously to make these credit operations possible, the international value of each of our currencies must be stabilized, otherwise the credits granted would deteriorate greatly in value or become exorbitant for the debtor if in the interval between the time of making the loan and its repayment, certain currencies depreciated.

It is not indispensable that the same currency be established for the whole continent. A fixed value, guaranteed by stabilization funds, would give the same result. The best type of exchange is one stabilized by balanced credits and debits for each nation. It would be absolutely necessary to come to an international agreement that existing tariffs and the relative values of the currencies could not be altered without the general consent of the American nations.

International trade, developed along the lines indicated, would be a beacon of hope for all America. Until now it has been a maxim that trade follows the flag. This is true, but to this principle must be added an American amendment that justice, too, follows the flag.

To sum up, the basis needed for American ideals is the defense of the standard of living of the people of America. What the United States has achieved in its vast territory, and in each of the units comprising it, should be achieved in the twenty-one nations of United America.

The following words of Carleton Beals have the strength of prophecy: "Idle factories and idle men never won fair peace. Men ill-housed and ill-fed have no country for which to fight. Our fields must flourish, our ships must run, our wheels must hum. On this depends our prosperity, perhaps even our institutions and domestic tranquility."

We must elevate the economic possibilities of each man as a producer and as a consumer, for upon this depends his dignity as a citizen of his country and of the world. Within the limits of the American continent, we must not permit the competition of merchandise which comes tainted with starvation wages, and we must make available to every home the benefits of industrial civilization, not merely to guarantee the well-being and liberty of the American man, but also to stimulate social justice and hold up to shame the exploitation of peoples in the rest of the world.

Redemption of the Masses · XV

OVER A GREAT EXPANSE, LATIN AMERICA IS AN archipelago of human groups surrounded by jungles and deserts. A considerable number of these groups have only the slightest contact with the others. They live in abject poverty and primitive ignorance. They have only what the earth brings forth, under the most rudimentary cultivation, to care for their needs. They are peoples on the point of death. Other elements live without being able to obtain work, or only with great difficulty, at starvation wages and in appalling conditions, with no economic guarantees whatsoever, the victims of every form of exploitation.

We all realize that the situation of these masses is the negation and the shame of civilization. It is not man alone who is their oppressor; it is nature, too. They live in a hostile world. The centuries of struggle of the human spirit to redeem itself have passed them by without leaving a trace.

This ignorance and isolation constitute one of the most degrading forms of slavery. The millions of families in America, living this sub-human life in one form or other, should be the object of the deep concern of the present leaders of affairs. It is their duty, in this dramatic moment of humanity's struggle, to transform the living conditions of the great neglected masses of this continent.

Man's freedom in the world of reality may be measured by his opportunity to apply himself to the work for which he is best fitted or likes best, and also by the returns he receives from his work for the satisfaction of his material and spiritual needs. Man feels himself free, and is free, when he knows that he has the same opportunity as the next man and that, according to his efforts, his aptitudes and his conduct, he can obtain all any other can. Men are free when they have access to schools, factories, business, social and intellectual circles, and when they know that by a reasonable amount of work they can acquire those things that make life pleasant, secure and healthful.

Despite all the fine phrases in their political constitutions, the illiterate inhabitants of our poverty-stricken, tropical countries are nothing but miserable slaves—undernourished, ravaged by malaria, hook worm and intestinal parasites; powerless against climate and epidemics. Denied the recreations that make life agreeable, they take refuge in alcohol and idleness. Yoked to the wooden plow that was their father's before them and will be their son's, they feel that under such conditions neither their own life nor that of their fellow-men means anything, since it is worth so little.

If wages in the countries of America were raised so their standard of living could be on a similar plane, it would foster an ennobling sense of equality. Not only would the inhabitants of this continent feel themselves free, but each would be a good consumer and a capable producer who would look upon his work as a contribution to the well-being and happiness of all.

But, it may be asked, can the Latin American nations, except for a favored few, so backward and neglected, work out their redemption, freedom and social welfare if left to their own resources? To answer this affirmatively would be to be blind to the realities that surround us. Even assuming that each nation could take all the time it needed for its own evolution, it would have to go through the centuries of slavery, adversity and sufferings that countless generations have endured.

Experience has shown us that during a century and a half of independence, and despite the great material resources of some of our nations, the ascent has been slow and difficult, beset with reverses and conflicts. The lack of geographical and climatic advantages and of natural resources, which might have greatly shortened the cultural cycles that must be passed through to achieve freedom, has obliged nations to struggle against elemental forces that could not be overcome. They have lacked the technique, capital, communications and the backing of a flourishing agriculture for their industrial development. It is not because of the inferiority of our nations, but because of the unbridgeable gulf between the resources at man's command and his indomitable surroundings.

To hope that man can be redeemed without putting at his service all the conquests science has achieved and applied over centuries is the idle dream of a visionary or the insensate promise of a demagogue. It will be a stroke of fortune for those countries, left to themselves and struggling on unequal terms against their overwhelming surroundings, to shake off the yoke of nature which has enslaved them like the most despotic tyrant and assemble their scattered forces, bring together their anarchic possibilities, and interchange their resources and their cultures for the benefit of all.

The objectives we have described as being beneficial to Latin America will likewise be of great value to a highly industrialized country such as the United States to maintain its economic prosperity, its social well-being and its spiritual values. The development of a civilization in the whole continent of America will constitute one outlet more among those counted upon by the United States in the international field, through which may flow the great concentrations of accumulated capital which hamper the progress of a new economy in that country.

Everyone agrees that the bases of capitalism as it has hitherto existed are not adequate to maintain economic prosperity. The recurring crises of the past are no longer able, no matter how costly the cataclysm, to initiate a new cycle of prosperity after depression. The process is a familiar one. After a catastrophic crisis that marks the end of a cycle of prosperity, the community suffers disastrous liquidations: the wiping out of capital or its reduction in value, the decline and loss of profits and savings which mark the final depths of the depression. But production is kept going by new capital which, though curtailed and decimated, has managed to survive the storm, and by new organizations which, by cutting costs, get under way and begin to afford opportunities for work and wages which increase the purchasing power of the community and thus set in motion the beginnings of a new cycle of prosperity.

But in every one of these crises the United States has suffered there have been factors which have stimulated the economic expansion and the progress of the reconstruction, such as the advance toward the West which was marked by vast investments in railroads and in every means of communication, the opening up of new farm lands, of mines, new industries and new cities. With this went a rapid increase in population and, as a result, the birth of colossal industries such as, first, the railroads; then the petroleum, meat-packing, electrical and movie industries, great factories to produce automobiles and all kinds of household equipment, stoves, washing machines, refrigerators, electric ranges and radios, which form an indispensable part of the material civilization of the United States.

Many believe that these opportunities for new investments have disappeared because the saturation point has been reached and because the population is not growing at the rapid pace of the last century. The cities have reached a static point in their growth, and the great industries have approached the limit of their expansion. The same is true of agricultural investments. All these circumstances, as well as the discouraging experience of the last war with respect to loans and investments made in Europe—ten billion dollars of war debts never paid—are the cause of the skepticism over the possibility that the same economic factors of expansion that have saved capitalism in other critical moments will work when this conflagration is over.

As opposed to this pessimism, and recognizing that for capitalism as it has existed there must be substituted some more efficient method of restoring permanent prosperity, we should not lose sight of the fact that the future can count on highly significant factors. What more marvelous opportunity to utilize all our surplus energy, not only accumulated capital but technique, enterprise, and initiative, than the construction of the continent of America! There may be no opportunity to build new railroads in the United States, but to the South are 30,000,000 square kilometers which need railroads and highways to cross this vast expanse. A new method of communication is slated for gigantic development: aviation. A new industry will soon make its appearance alongside the vast automobile industry, that of the small low-priced airplane for the person of average means. The same is true of the manufacture of transport planes. And the great investments for the development of thousands of cities and the exploitation and sanitation of vast tropical farmlands! The great resources required for a planned industrialization!

The advance toward the West will become the advance of collaboration toward the South. It will not be the movement of settlers, for the United States is not over-populated. It will be the movement of economic forces to create on the basis of all the resources of all our lands, a healthy expansion which will establish the reciprocal prosperity of our nations.

The United States hopes to maintain the extraordinary standard of living it has created. Latin America is trying to establish a standard of living which it has not yet known. The pooling of our economies and our resources will achieve this common end, the economic salvation of Latin America and the maintenance of the high standard of living of the United States. From this fruitful combination will come a united, fraternal Continent. These goals cannot be regarded from the point of view of countries separate and antagonistic in their international dealings. We must act in the spirit of a federation of nations. We are marching toward an indissoluble mingling of our destinies, and only by establishing the economic unity of America can we erect full solidarity upon a permanent basis.

M *Under What Social Banner?* · XVI

AN'S MOST CHERISHED DREAM, THE WIPING out of poverty forever, is no longer hampered by the all-powerful hostility of Nature. Modern technology, which astonishes and moves us by its growing progress, puts at the disposition of constructive intelligence the instruments necessary to dominate the resources and forces of Nature. Production in abundance is within the grasp of civilization, and it is necessary only to direct it to make it inseparable from liberty.

Man no longer has any need to enslave man. He has slaves at his command: machines. To construct the world of liberty and justice which all mankind looks forward to, it is necessary only to put in play all the excess energy the modern world holds. The idle energy that is waiting to be used is enormous; it is to be found in the great masses of the unemployed who lack only the opportunity to work; in the great squandering of strength that comes from economic anarchy, speculation and disorder.

A fair distribution calls for abundant production. And modern technology can make this possible, not only through the raw materials which are to be found in abundance, but through substitutes and plastics which are being discovered every day in amazing, almost incredible forms.

Nylon is replacing silk. Glass can be made into flexible textiles and used advantageously, at times, instead of steel. Oil can be derived from coal, and rubber is being found in a great variety of products. It might be said that every day there is a revelation and a new force at work for the liberation of man.

The rate of production will grow in a geometric progression once peace comes. All the energies now devoted to war will be put to peace-time uses. The basic materials, such as plastics, which are being demanded in vast quantities for the many products essential in our modern civilization, can be supplied by numerous agricultural products. Technology is mankind's great redeemer of today.

Statistics show that there are in the world 2,300 corporations or laboratories which employ 70,000 scientists and technicians. They are discovering new secrets which at the moment are largely employed for destruction, but which will be useful later on for the construction of the world of tomorrow. The scientific methods being applied in agriculture are producing equally marvelous results.

Thomas More, more than four centuries ago, foretold that, with good organization, men would need to work only two or three hours a day to satisfy the needs of a civilized life. In any case, it is a recognized fact that if all the technical capacity for producing and for adapting production to the organized needs of the community were fully employed, then with fewer hours of work than at present and merely by putting into play the conquests and discoveries of modern science, all would achieve a state of well-being far superior to that enjoyed by most civilized countries today.

But all these astounding powers which man commands to build a new civilization must be well understood. Man must have a clear idea of the direction in which he is going. Without wise organization, the enterprise may fall into errors, make shifts and disastrous experiences which would lead first to suffering and disillusion on the part of the people and then swiftly to violence and despair that would end in the most sinister dictatorship. All the doctrinary explosives that might wreck the peace must be rendered harmless before they can do their damage. The dissatisfaction and the anarchy of thought which ravaged the world after the last war, and which were worse than the war itself, must not be repeated because of lack of forethought and intelligent planning.

Fortunately the statesmen, specialists and thinkers of the democratic nations are preparing to make ample provision for social justice in the post-war world. At the same time the workers' organizations, which will play a decisive role in the future, are daily acquiring a greater sense of responsibility. The International Labor Conference which met in New York in 1941 gave a brilliant account not only of the extraordinary achievements of the organization but of the clear orientation of the workers with regard to post-war reconstruction. At this Congress the principle of collaboration as a means to saving the peace and making it permanent was upheld.

The most terrible mistake that could be made would be to attempt to put these powerful instruments for abolishing poverty under characteristic despotic systems. This would be to commit the blunder—in order to prevent the privileged few from reaping the benefits of applied science—of merely handing over to new minorities the exploitation of the gains of mankind's many centuries of effort.

It is a serious problem to know clearly under what device this new continental civilization is to develop. Is the dictatorship of the proletariat to be the guide to the new paths of world economy? Or is it perhaps Nazism, with its system of complete and forcible control of man and conscience and its racial oppression, which is to inspire the new school of economic thought? Will the old capitalist system endure?

Without going into an examination of these possibilities, which lies outside the purpose of this book, we can state with all conviction that mankind will reject these three forms which have not only failed materially, but have torn to shreds the moral life and happiness of the world. All three systems stand for the negation of human liberty. Nazism and Marxist Communism represent the regimentation of the conscience that turns man into a robot without will or rights. Capitalism, as it has existed, has been the breeding-ground of immense privileges, and of discontent and poverty among the masses. With its inevitable recurring economic crises, unemployment and misery, we ask, in view of these inequalities, whether anything regiments the spirit more than insecurity and hunger.

Marxism, great as a source of inspiration for justice, but unable to produce a just social organization, aims to end the privileges of private property in order to maintain economic equality. Even if this could be done, this impossible ideal would be substituted with a privilege even more serious and dangerous for human dignity and happiness: the privilege of power.

Reflection and reality teach us that a dictatorship established to uphold forcibly a system of supposed equality is never exercised by the proletariat. Under this misleading abstract label, it is men of flesh and blood who take over the power, a power concentrated exclusively in a tyrannical minority and totally and absolutely non-existent for the great majority whose sole function is to obey. Man longs for economic security, but his aversion to tyranny and irresponsible authority is just as profound. Equality of political power among the masses means a step toward the realization of economic equality and security through the will of the majority. Without the distribution of this political power to the masses, all the promises of economic equality are dependent upon the whim of the men in power.

Nazism is not even worth refuting. It aggravates all the ills of despotism and, besides, who would want to live in prison, under the arrogance of Aryan jailers with their self-assigned superiority and mission of dominating the world?

Neither does classic liberalism constitute an adequate system. The concentration of wealth—which seems an unavoidable law of the system's mechanism—leads to the choking up of the channels of economic freedom. Its free functioning is hampered by barriers and a lack of adaptation to the active forces which animate modern progress. The greatest obstacle in its path is the monopoly, the trust, which implies the most flagrant contradiction with the free play of economic factors on which its vitality depends.

Monopoly is the negation of free competition, free prices and a free market. It falsifies the whole economic system. It utilizes the achievements of technology, which would produce more cheaply under free competition, to make greater profits. With profit as its only objective, monopoly weakens the market with its high prices and, entrenched in the security of its special privileges, unjustly thrusts all the risks upon the little business men, who must struggle against each other.

The natural forces which theoretically should automatically adjust the ups and downs of the economic process, are slowed down and obstructed in their action by monopoly, by the unavoidable concentrations of the capitalist system. This system has lost its resiliency during its great crises. Its power to rejuvenate itself is gone, and it can no longer rise miraculously like the Phoenix from its own ashes.

The capitalist system does not work because it is impossible to prolong the spiral of production indefinitely with profit as the sole stimulus. Under this system, a large share of the dividends and profits which are the fruit of production pile up and constitute the investment reserve needed to keep the economy in motion. The capital actually in circulation at a given moment is constant and is distributed in salaries (which constitute the consuming ability of the public), in dividends and in interest. The new reserve capital swiftly increases the volume of production. As long as this volume keeps abreast of the purchasing power of the consumer, prosperity is maintained. But as prosperity grows, the large profits and high rates of interest increase the amount of reserve capital at the expense of the purchasing power of the community. The accumulated capital that cannot find an outlet in investment increases costs and raises prices so that the consuming power is unable to absorb the goods produced under these conditions. This inability to consume increases until the critical moment when the markets become saturated. The flood begins with the closing of the factories, unemployment and all the other dreadful consequences of depression.

What has taken place under this process? Has there been over-production? This idea is instantly refuted by the irony of vast multitudes manifestly in dire need. The thing that has paralyzed the working of the system and unleashed economic disaster, is not the lack of need on the part of the community; it is the lack of profits on the part of the investors. The desire for profit has stopped the machinery.

This human stimulus to action, left to itself, has not been able to respond to the real needs of a community wasting away and suffering from lack of abundant production. Is any further proof needed that the capitalist system has broken down like a worn-out machine before the world's astonished and anxious eyes? Fantastic potential technical resources, a super-abundance of capital and unlimited consumer power are paralyzed. And what is it that has produced this failure under apparent economic liberty? To a great extent it is the flagrant contradiction of unbridled economic freedom leading to the carefully controlled arbitrariness of the trusts.

The need to re-establish this violated liberty is one of the motives that underlies the intervention of the modern state. It has been necessary to combat concentrations and monopolies which destroy the bases of economic liberty. Moreover, not only must the great existing concentrations of wealth be attacked, but also the factors which produce them. Excessive profits must be done away with, dividends and interest cut, thus eliminating disproportionate returns and helping to avoid the crises that are produced by the accumulation of investment capital at the cost of the consumer's purchasing power.

Other fundamental reasons for the intervention of the state in the rapid restoration or re-establishment of the lost equilibrium of economic life, are the complexity of modern life, the wide distribution of population, and the urgent need to satisfy the implacable demands of the great human masses that exist today. For these the automatic interplay of economic forces at times becomes slow and unsatisfactory. The blind determinism upon which classic capitalism relied took no account of human values. The need to satisfy collective justice, which cannot be left to insensible mechanical forces and fatalistic operations having no connection with the palpitating human life they are made for, demands the intervention of the state, to replace the dehumanized features of uncontrolled economic chance. This must be done to meet the growing and multiple clamor of the necessities, the privations and adversity that man suffers on his earthly journey.

Actually the periodic economic crises are safety valves through which surpluses are eliminated. The readjustment takes place through a painful series of operations and liquidations until a balance is re-established; but meanwhile the elements ground to bits are not just mechanisms; they are men, homes, communities. If when left to their own laws, economic forces lead to upsets, disturbances and bankruptcy, who is to act as intervenor to avoid these fatal disorders and at the same time confirm man in the enjoyment of his essential rights? Only the state can restore the balance and maintain progress under the sign of a production which has as its fundamental basis the needs of the community and not merely the dominating lust for profits. This should be carried out by the State indirectly by taxing excess profits of surplus capital, and investing the return in public works, thus increasing the opportunities for work and eliminating the excess accumulation of investment capital unable to find an outlet at a given moment, one of the factors that upset the capitalistic machine.

As regards our continent, it will be of supreme importance for its future destiny and for its economic development that the measures of economic control we have indicated function most strongly at those points where most wealth is concentrated. Hence, in our still virgin or only slightly developed regions, legitimate profits and fair returns of interest are still real working incentives for the vast amounts of capital that can be absorbed there. Without encouraging exorbitant profits, private initiative can and should be allowed legitimate gains to accelerate the pace of building the new America.

The intervention of the State should, as we have pointed out, take an indirect form, because if it becomes a producer itself and assumes the control of production, eliminating the spirit of free enterprise and private initiative, liberty will be endangered. To avoid this we must supersede traditional capitalism, with its concentration of wealth and its excess profits which work to the detriment of the community, yet preserve liberalism's initiative, its spirit of enterprise, by doing away with great fortunes and promoting the widespread creation of small ones.

It is enlightening to observe how the Nazi organization plays up to all social groups: the worker, because of control over the capitalist class; capital, because through the single party system the workers are kept under thumb; the consumer, because the planned economy keeps watch over the quality and prices of products.

Against this totalitarian new order, the democracies should plant a system which would not only satisfy all legitimate social interests, but in addition guarantee the priceless enjoyment of liberty. To be sure, this system is still in the process of creation; but the cardinal points of its content are firmly fixed.

What is to be the ideological thesis on which the proposition of maintaining social justice and liberty is to be based? The absolute control of production, distribution and prices? Then we fall into totalitarianism, because if we begin to set up controls along every step of productive activity, we shall soon discover that our liberties have vanished.

The great qualities which come from initiative, the spirit of enterprise, individual responsibility in creative activity, to which democracy owes its material prosperity and its great moral victories, would cease to exist, and once abolished they would have to be replaced with forced labor, regimentation and blind obedience. The price would be the sacrifice of all liberties. And to attempt to set up controls over the whole economic process is as stupid as to attempt to substitute nature in sending out the sap from the roots of the forest trees.

Many are the problems involved in a system of economic justice. Modern technology makes large scale enterprise and mass production necessary in certain fields. Great plants, which have the advantage of simplifying and rapidly turning out low-cost products, make possible a system of abundance. To destroy this advantage is to forego one of the achievements of applied science. In this reality lies one of the many contradictions of our economic existence: abundance side by side with concentration of wealth. This great centralization, so necessary for large-scale production, must not be allowed to foster trusts or private monopolies. In many cases a good solution would be to carry on these enterprises through co-operatives or with mixed control, in which the government, private owners and the workers' organizations would participate. But it must never be lost sight of that the world needs big production and what must be assured is that this production shall not depend on profits destined for the exclusive privilege of the few, while from below, the masses reach up their poverty-wasted hands in a futile plea for the goods produced.

The world still lives in the realm of ideological battles. It is far from having found the main highway where all purposes converge. We want liberty, the end of imperialism, the abolition of poverty, the suppression of war, but the path by which to reach these aspirations is still obscure. We know of a few negative experiences, as for example, the evil of all violent methods—the Soviet systems under constant revision; the Volstead Act in the United States; the permanent surrender of public administration to the management of private business, which produces results contrary to liberty and successful administration. On the other hand, in startling contrast to the foregoing, the experiences and emergency measures of the New Deal will impose unimpeachable standards of planned economy in the post-war reorganization. Persistently the democratic governments have also been invading the field of private initiative. In the first place, the great public utility concerns can no longer operate under a system of private enterprise.

Next, those industries which, because of lack of stability or because of their magnitude, can no longer find sufficient impulse except through government administration, have been delivering themselves over to the state. Similarly, industries swiftly expanded to gigantic proportions by the needs of armed defense, can no longer survive exclusively on the basis of private initiative. All these fields of action have been succumbing before the invasion of the state. The control that the latter has consolidated over finance, credit, foreign commerce and money is a powerful indirect instrumentality of invasion that never ceases. The collective methods put in practice during the war, undoubtedly will have a major influence when peace arrives. Above all, the example of England in knowing how to maintain a highly controlled economy together with the enjoyment of a freedom greater than that permitted in the last war, will be an impressive factor in the forthcoming reorganization of the world.

The tumultuous current of hasty methods will pass away, and the ardent desire to combine social justice with the enjoyment of freedom will turn economic life back into its proper channel: that which leads to the wiping out of poverty by means of just distribution.

In the fog that covers the landscape can be discerned a pacific and democratic solution: let the state permanently take over the just distribution of the people's wealth. The production and circulation of wealth would thus, in general terms, remain in the hands of private initiative except for the control required for social welfare; but once the economic process has been carried through along free lines—with safeguards against the formation of concentration of economic power which might challenge the state's supremacy, and while preserving the creative privilege of initiative, the spirit of enterprise and individual responsibility—the state, in the final stage, distribution, must level off the inequalities occasioned by this process. Such a system would guarantee labor's conquests which humanize and dignify work, would give technicians, investors and entrepreneurs the opportunity to make use of their creative abilities; and in the last stage of the process, the distribution of profits, could utilize the surplus to promote useful activities on a non-profit basis to do away with unemployment and protect defenseless human beings and homes from avoidable forms of adversity.

In this way the maintenance of a living wage can be guaranteed, as well as proper sanitation, education, recreation, and medical care in factories and farms. All these services will represent a definite increase in the worker's share of the returns from production. How is this equitable distribution to be accomplished? Chiefly by utilizing two great levers the democratic state has at its disposal: the income tax or its equivalents, which draw off excess profits into the state treasury, and public works. In addition to augmenting the possibility of employment in accordance with the needs of the nation, public works increasingly provide opportunities for economic security, cultural advancement, recreation and health for the whole nation, thus increasing the actual amount of wealth distributed to each person.

Under these conditions the inequalities of wealth cease to be important. Once the state has laid the bases of equity and organization in its role as distributor, the important thing is not the amount of capital, but of earnings. If the latter are so distributed that nobody has a surplus which prevents a fair share for all, what difference do inequalities of wealth make?

As a matter of fact, the inequalities of wealth are being combated, not by depriving a person of the amount of money he possesses, but by sharply reducing his returns and his privileges.

Economic security, insurance against unemployment, sickness and old age, must be looked upon as a crusade, a ceaseless effort. In Latin America, especially, because of its poverty, its lack of social spirit and its predominant individualism, man is the prey of the direst adversity. Sickness, unemployment and the loss of father or husband, take place in the face of shocking community indifference. We are far from the noble concept that in the hour of trial a man should find the helping hand of his country.

When one thinks of such discoveries as the photo-electric cell, which makes possible the remote control of a number of industries which no longer require man's direct intervention, one reaches the conclusion that a new change in man's right to existence is coming into being. One of the great realities of modern economy is the ever greater return per man per hour. This means that as technology advances the opportunities for work diminish. As a result, the rights of man must increase along the democratic paths that humanity is following. He has a right to live decently, even if he, through no fault of his own, lacks the opportunity to work. This fact has serious connotations for the future, one of which is that it will not be principally the workers' organizations but the broad aggregate of consumers that will play the most important role in social justice.

The system of "relief" or its equivalents, in those cases where normal economy has not been able to provide opportunities for work, must be continued by the State as a right of the individual and not as a favor. It must come quickly and efficiently before hunger and despair have put their blot of shame on a social organization which we claim to have built up in the name of Christian civilization with sentiments of solidarity among all men.

When this program takes in a whole continent, a continent that still possesses vast virgin territories, then we can appreciate how great are the program and its possibilities. A system of this sort would give the assurance of abundance and would satisfy, together with the desire for liberty, the longing for justice.

T

HUS FAR I HAVE DISCUSSED THE POSSIBILITIES
of the political, economic, cultural, even the biological rehabilitation of the American man. In this book, we have seen
him, first, overwhelmed by the violence of the Conquest; then
enslaved, in his human relationships, by the rigors of the
colonial period; and in his productive life, by imperialistic
capitalism—but ever moving unswervingly toward liberty
along the paths of democracy and continental co-operation.

We have considered his greatness and his servitude; the vast
untouched resources that Nature puts before him; the moral
strength that his homogeneous civic institutions give him; the
weakness that his haphazard technical preparation and the
unfair distribution of the wealth he has produced imposes
upon him. We have also analyzed the hopes that inspire the
happy union of his most articulate political ideals: that of
the North, "America for the Americans," defined by Monroe
in a doctrine that has gained in equity as it has evolved from
a unilateral into a many-sided and collective principle; and
that of the South, consecrated in the thesis of Bolivar, "America for the World," an aspiration no longer merely a fine phrase,
in view of the sacrifices the nations of this hemisphere are
making to help all the countries of the globe, without geographic or racial distinction, to create universal peace.

And we also have seen that the nations of America, throughout their history, have demonstrated their determination to
be free and to maintain their sovereignty.

In the extended pages of this volume, we have been eyewitnesses of many splendid undertakings and of many mistakes
and sufferings. But never for one moment have we lost sight
of the universal determination of the American man, and this
will be the determination that will make itself felt at the end
of the war and afterward, when the time comes to construct
a world community that will guarantee the harmony of all and
the rights of each, the security of the whole and the legitimate
aspirations of the parts.

It would be premature to outline in all its details the world of tomorrow. But one thing is already clear: isolation will be absolutely impossible.

We are moving toward general co-ordination, toward international collaboration, which will open up new paths of work and triumph—but which also will impose new obligations. And to fulfill these obligations, undoubtedly the national states will have to curtail voluntarily certain of their rights as such.

At the present stage of the world's development, the principle of the sovereignty of states constitutes the firmest groundwork of international organization. Sovereignty is to the community as liberty is to man: a fundamental right which may not, because of its very nature, emanate from an alien will, and without the exercise of which none of the conditions indispensable for the true development of a country can be realized.

Through exercise of its sovereignty, a nation is provided with the institutions its people desire. Through exercise of its sovereignty, a nation enacts its own laws, defends its territory, declares and wages war, concludes alliances, signs treaties, accredits and receives diplomatic and consular representatives, in a word, orders its own existence and co-ordinates it with that of others on a footing of juridical equality, mutual respect and harmonious creative collaboration.

In this broad sense, sovereignty is independence. As such, it represents the characteristic attribute of the state. The present stage of dwelling together of the nations may therefore be defined as "the degree of balance of sovereignties." An upset of this balance implies the appearance of disorder, sooner or later ending in violence.

It follows that whoever aims to eliminate war as a means of settling controversies between peoples must begin by strengthening the safeguards surrounding the sovereign, free and independent action of their governments.

This is the classic thesis. On it, the political life of the American democracies has rested. To uphold it we have not only made incalculable sacrifices, but also have endured a whole succession of struggles and privations and have put forth efforts which are an index to the majesty of our destinies. In some cases they have led us to participate in conflicts which apparently had no connection with our future.

It must, however, be pointed out that this crystal clear concept, which today seems incontrovertible, has not existed at all times in the past. The very word "sovereignty" as understood today was not included in the vocabulary of political theories until quite recently. So far as is known, it was Bodin who first used it, in 1577, in his treatise on "Republics." He then broadened the meaning which the word carried during the Middle Ages, when its sole connotation was to define the capacities of a monarch, or of some great lord who recognized no higher authority in his field of action than his own.

Concepts, like peoples, are subject to change. They are the fruits of creative imagination, which adapts the thinking machinery of the individual or of the human group to the temporary and variable reality of events. If they become fixed and rigid, paralysis ensues. Immobility is an admission of automatism. And automatism of concepts is more deplorable when its existence permanently stifles any alteration. But permanent metamorphosis explains the modifications which the principle of the sovereignty of states has undergone through the centuries.

Pufendorf, in *De Jure Naturae et Gentium,* laid down the rule that sovereignty is not an all-embracing and unrestricted power. In fact, the sovereignty of a nation must, if it is active, be limited to itself. This limitation is contained in the political institutions of the peoples.

But there is more to it than this. During the eighteenth century sovereignty admittedly was neither uniform nor homogeneous. Confederations of states stressed the need of distinguishing between the total sovereignty of the whole and the relative sovereignty of the component members. Throughout the nineteenth century, moreover, and still more after the First World War, statesmen gradually adopted a more flexible and human interpretation.

In 1932, a distinguished former Rumanian Minister of Foreign Affairs, M. Titulescu, asked: "Does the sovereignty of states constitute an obstacle to peace?" His answer was in the affirmative. In fact, unlimited sovereignty must necessarily lead us constantly to wars. The whole of international law, founded on the doctrine of sovereignty, would automatically cease to exist if sovereignty were not voluntarily confined within certain limits. Such limits do exist, and are called treaties. Thanks to them, two or more governments are able to subordinate their own individual rights to obtain a balance, either economic or political. Examples are agreements regulating commerce, tariffs, armament reductions, the common use of boundary water-ways, etc. Every such agreement specifically curtails freedom of action.

We thus find ourselves in the presence of a situation outwardly paradoxical: without sovereignty there can be no international law; yet in practice the notion of unrestricted sovereignty would overthrow order in the world. Alive to the seriousness of this, a French jurist, Le Fur, wrote: "To reconcile the sovereignty of the state with the rights of the international community is the crucial problem of Foreign Public Law."

The solution lies in a happy mean, similar to that which has made life within each country possible. The independence of the individual is indispensable to the welfare of the community; but the community would disappear if that individual independence were not organized in accordance with a system of legal and moral restrictions. Similarly, the sovereignty of every member is a basic requirement of international society, yet collective peace and progress require a partial voluntary relinquishment of separate national rights. The secret does not lie in the incompatible extremes of either absolute independence or complete submission, but in the reciprocity of mutual dependence.

Because this concept has not prevailed, the history of nations has been an endless series of cruel struggles and deceptive and transitory appeasements. Sovereignty, appealed to by the weak in the hour of defense, is seized upon by the powerful as a weapon when they launch their onslaught. We find a similar phenomenon in natural history. The same substance which makes the defensive armament of the tortoise, serves also for the lion's paw.

This leads us to an examination of the essence of rights. Man has a natural proclivity to consider every matter from the standpoint exclusively of its advantage to him. The result is that he instinctively tends to stress his rights, which are a benefit, and to neglect his duties, which imply an obligation. However, both ethically and politically there is not a single right that does not involve an immediate and accompanying duty. Social facts are like coins which bear on their obverse the effigy of something pleasant—skill, security, abundance—while on the reverse we see the austere figure of duty. Each side justifies and supplements the other. Even the most celebrated of all democratic proclamations—the Declaration of the Rights of Man and of the Citizen—is largely conceived in the form of prohibitions, constituting a defensive safeguard for the individual against the power of the community.

Man is free, not because of the truth of Rousseau's romantic theory based on an erroneous assumption as to the original liberty of the "happy savage," but because society—without which the life of the individual is inconceivable—grants him that liberty in exchange for a series of checks and curbs that subordinate his actions to a common ideal.

In the "state of nature" spoken of in the *Contrat Social,* each one was entitled to possess whatever he could win by his own strength. Even under a collective scheme of existence we have not wholly succeeded in emancipating ourselves from that situation of disorder and uncertainty. Might is right. And when the stronger does not gain his end by force of arms, he resorts to the artifices of diplomacy or achieves it by means of economic imperialism, through abusive use of his superior wealth.

Since, in Hobbes' words, man is still a wolf, to remedy this evil, only one legitimate means occurs to the mind of the investigator: to limit and co-ordinate sovereignties. Such limitation may be effected in either of two ways. It may be done by main force, the method advocated by the totalitarians. Or it may be done through the acceptance of an international superstructure, such as that aimed at by the free nations united under the glorious canopy of democracy.

History teaches us that, up to the present, both these procedures have failed. But while greed for power has failed because of congenital and natural incapacity, there is nothing to prove that humanity is fundamentally unable to achieve through collaboration and justice that which no empire has yet succeeded in gaining enduringly through arbitrary power and violence. In contrast, the repeated defeats suffered by imperialism are clear proof that peoples cannot be co-ordinated by a conqueror.

The cohesion which Hitler dreams of imposing on Europe as a basis for the general servitude of all the continents under the heel of Pan-Germanism is neither new nor original. Before the wizard of Berchtesgaden embarked upon that adventure, other men, much more logically minded than he—Alexander, Caesar and Charlemagne, to say nothing of Charles V and Napoleon—had attempted to unify the known world by force.

Three of these rulers, Alexander the Great, Caesar and Napoleon, started from a clearly Mediterranean conception of culture. The universe, in their opinion, ought to revolve around the idea which Greece or Rome or Paris (the latter as a synthesis of Græco-Latin evolution) had formed of civilization and of the role of man. In the case of the other two—Charlemagne and, centuries later, Charles V—their aspirations after unity were from the outset vitiated by a somber Gothic frenzy. In it the historian may, without undue effort, detect the stifling moral fogginess of the Germanic way of being. All five of them, however, left the same ruin behind them. And their action, which was directed at forging a powerful union of territories and institutions, ended by promoting a vast process of dissolution. Alexander's career signals the end of the Hellenic period. The exploits of Julius Caesar mark the peak of Rome's upward course; after it came the decline that paved the way for the barbarian invasion. Charlemagne's empire disintegrated at Verdun; Charles the Fifth's in Westphalia. And Napoleon's was wrecked in the flames of Moscow, the snows of the Berezna and the shell-scarred walls of Zaragosa.

Hitler's adventure is still under way. But who doubts the eventual fate of this latest megalomaniac? However imposing the victories won so far by the Nazi armies may seem, their defeat is only a matter of time.

Imperialistic efforts, often tried, have invariably ended disastrously. Per contra, we may assert that world conciliation has never yet been tried in a properly integrated way. Even the League of Nations was not participated in by all the countries. Its failure to achieve the expected degree of success was certainly not because the fundamental idea was vague or impracticable. It was designed for universal action, but very soon, by the force of events, it became a European association. Some few states in the Americas, Asia and Africa were also present, but symbolically rather than otherwise.

The fact that the decline of the League of Nations coincided with the rise of Nazism and Fascism goes to prove that the course recommended by those statesmen who were erroneously criticized as "Versailles idealists" was after all the one and only path. Further proof is that the purposes defined now by the democracies in the midst of their struggles in behalf of freedom's future, square absolutely with the ideals of the League, as witness the Atlantic Charter, signed August 14, 1941, by President Roosevelt and Prime Minister Churchill, which contains the following declarations:

1—Their countries seek no aggrandizement, territorial or other;

2—They desire to see no territorial changes that do not accord with the expressed wishes of the people concerned;

3—They respect the right of all peoples to choose the form of government under which they will live; and they wish to see sovereign right and self-government restored to those who have been forcibly deprived of them;

4—They will endeavor, with due respect for their existing obligations, to further the enjoyment by all states, great or small, victor or vanquished, of access on equal terms to the trade and to the raw materials of the world which are needed for their economic prosperity;

5—They desire to bring about the fullest collaboration between all nations in the economic field with the object of securing for all improved labor standards, economic advancement and social security;

6—After the final destruction of the Nazi tyranny, they hope to see established a peace which will afford to all nations the means of dwelling in safety within their own boundaries and which will afford assurance that all the men in all the lands may live out their lives in freedom from fear and want;

7—Such a peace should enable all men to traverse the high seas and oceans without hindrance.

8—They believe that all of the nations of the world, for realistic as well as spiritual reasons, must come to the abandonment of the use of force. Since no future peace can be maintained if land, sea or air armaments continue to be employed by nations which threaten or may threaten aggression outside of their frontiers, they believe, pending the establishment of a wider and permanent system of general security that the disarmament of such nations is essential. They will likewise aid and encourage all other practicable measures which will lighten for peace-loving peoples the crushing burden of armaments.

To make these propositions a reality, the free peoples must be morally and materially united during the war. The world's destiny is being forged on the Russian front, in Australia, in China, India, Africa and the Pacific. But through the darkness that still envelops us, we can see the daybreak of a new era.

Even so, we would be making a fatal mistake if we thought that the peace, when the hour of victory comes, is going to be any less difficult to win than the war itself. The world, utterly exhausted and famished, will have to be reconstructed and kept alive. On the wreckage we shall have to set to work to erect the splendid new freedom of tomorrow. The task will be long and hard, calling for ceaseless and determined effort. Trade, industry and agriculture will have to be organized on a basis entirely different from that which kept the world in unbalance in the illusory and compromise peace period after the last war.

Yes, the task will be long, its material difficulties incalculable. To undertake it successfully, it will be necessary that every nation sacrifice some of that aggressive pride which has distorted the notion of sovereignty.

It is absurd to believe that in a world which has achieved such stupendous material progress as ours, there can prevail a threatening, uncompromising, aggressive autarchy that blocks the co-ordinated action of the states in behalf of the general welfare, and in the last analysis, of universal peace itself.

The new order, which will arise from this terrible conflagration will not, of course, be Hitler's vandalic and sterile "new order," but one based on law, more elastic, yet stronger, an order in which all the states will have to collaborate by curtailing their individual ambitions, cutting down their armies, eliminating aggressiveness, and building up a system in which war is outlawed, in which differences between nations may be settled without suicidal resort to force.

Some kind of universal structure will have to be created, including a co-ordinating council on which all the nations are represented and which will act as a board of arbitration, as an international court of justice and as an official mediator in every conflict. But aside from this, it will be indispensable to give a new meaning to what we today term national sovereignty. In the future, no country may, as a function of its own independence, endanger the independence of others. The liberty of each shall be respected to the extent that it does not injure any other. But license to work evil will be curbed by moral, commercial, economic and legal sanctions which will render impossible the hegemony of any one state. In a world where sovereignties are unrestricted, the weak are at the mercy of the strong, and the latter, in turn, are exposed to the dangers involved in dividing up the loot. So long as equality of rights is not coupled with equality of opportunities and equal access to resources, the arbitrary dictum of unlimited sovereignty— like that of absolute liberty of the individual in domestic life —will benefit the powerful and give an advantage to the aggressive.

Now, in reality, there is no such thing as natural equity. States, therefore, if abandoned to the dialectical play of action and reaction, will invariably revert to inequality so long as no higher agency exists able to curb the stronger in favor of the weaker, and further, as between the powerful themselves, establish a clear and equitable balance. In enforcing international law, the most important sources of which are the moral sense of the peoples and the dispositions consecrated by treaties, that agency would serve as a shield for the rights of weak nations and to limit to the degree necessary, the ambition for pre-eminence of the powerful. No sovereignty would be diminished, merely co-ordinated with other sovereignties, just as in the democratic balance within a republic, the liberty of citizens is not reduced merely because they entrust the exercise of some of their rights to a central authority which acts on their behalf and sees to it that order is observed by all.

No disarmament, whether of armies or of the spirit, can be attained so long as the exaggerated notion of national sovereignty which prevailed throughout the nineteenth century and the early years of the twentieth is still entertained. Nor should we overlook the fact that it was by virtue of such an inordinate notion of sovereignty that Germany restored military service and re-occupied the Rhineland, that Mussolini took the diplomatic steps preceding the invasion of Ethiopia, and that the three dictatorships of Germany, Italy and Japan betrayed their international commitments and, breaking away from Geneva, combined to attack the whole of peace-loving humanity. Such cases must never be repeated.

Sovereignty, like liberty, must sacrifice part of its rights for the good of the whole. This war will have been a senseless waste of work, life and fortune if the first thing it achieves is not the creation of world interdependence which shall guarantee enduring and indivisible peace.

In 1933 the International Institute of Intellectual Cooperation conducted an inquiry into the best means of avoiding war. Professor Einstein, the mathematician, gave the following opinion: "In the interests of international security the state must be willing to give up a part of its freedom of action; in other words, it must accept a curtailment of its sovereignty."

Commenting on Einstein's statement, Dr. Sigmund Freud said: "Violence can be defeated only if power is transferred from the individual to a great united body which shares the same beliefs. It will not be possible to avoid war until men are willing to set up a central power with authority to settle all differences. For this two things are necessary: the creation of this supreme tribunal and its instrumentation with the power to enforce its decisions."

These lofty disinterested concepts of two of the most distinguished scientists of our day are those which, consciously or unconsciously, pervade public opinion in the democracies.

The Americas, because of their history, their nature, their common worship of liberty, are called upon to play a leading part in the work of conciliation necessary to the future interdependence of nations. The experience gained by inter-American conferences shows that continental understanding can be achieved without outside pressure. The settlement of the controversy between Colombia and Peru of 1933-35; of the conflict between Bolivia and Paraguay of 1928-35; and more recently, of the sharp difficulties between Ecuador and Peru, are evidence of the spirit of co-ordination which distinguishes our hemisphere. They recall Bolívar's happy phrase: "The New World should be constituted by free and independent nations, *united among themselves by a body of law common to all of them, to govern their foreign relations.*"

The control of which the Liberator spoke is not a step backward but forward along the road which will lead the nations to dwell together in a civilized community. We have seen how rights and duties supplement one another. In the future a higher principle will prevail over the idea of national sovereignty—as over the dogma of individual liberty—the idea of international collaboration. "In the notion of solidarity," wrote León Duguit, "the idea of liberty as right will disappear, to yield its place to liberty as a duty, liberty as a function of society." A century before Duguit stated his proposition, Auguste Comte had already outlined this fundamental principle: "The word *right* must be discarded from the genuine language of politics, just as the word *cause* should be dropped from the genuine language of philosophy. Every one has duties towards every one else and nobody has more than a single right: fully to perform his duty."

The American peoples understood this from the very hour of their emancipation. In his draft for a Declaration of the Rights of the People of Chile, Mariano Egaña, a patriot of that nation, stated in 1810 that it is exceedingly difficult for any nation, even by dint of great sacrifices, to maintain by itself its own isolated sovereignty. In the same vein, the Colombian Government, on April 17, 1823, announced that the time had come to set up a Pan-American confederation which would serve as a point of contact in the face of common danger, as well as interpret public treaties and act as a court of arbitration and conciliation of differences. This Colombian message imbued with the prevailing spirit of the period, foresaw an alliance and political confederation of the American states, both in peace and war, but it expressly stated that the confederation should not in any way interfere with the exercise of the sovereignty of the contracting parties. In theory this condition placed certain bounds on Simón Bolívar's original conception.

The scruple against contracting strictly juridical ties, and the idea that the union of the Americas should above all be the result of historical and cultural assimilation, also inspired a Brazilian, Oliveira Lima, when he said that such a union would in reality be "a natural manifestation of the cordiality existing between the different political members of a group of nations destined to integrate an association *lacking legal ties,* but bound by ethical duties all the stronger in that they flowed from a sense of collective responsibility emanating in turn from a sane and broad interpretation of human duties."

President Wilson, who also insisted this was the proper way to interpret inter-continental ties, defined Pan Americanism as a union of the American Republics in their capacity of spiritual allies, "that march in accord because they think alike and are animated by common sympathies and ideals."

Since the First World War, and more especially since the Inter-American Conference for the Maintenance of Peace held at Buenos Aires in 1936, this purely moral quality of Pan Americanism has been strengthened by practical commitments of a more solid and efficacious character. Two factors in particular promoted more rapid evolution: the Good Neighbor Policy, advocated and carried into effect by the administration of President Roosevelt, and the growing threat of the totalitarian powers.

The outstanding difference between Pan-American hopes of the nineteenth century and present day reality lies in the fact that the politicians of independence days sought continental unity as a counterpoise to European action, whereas the politicians of today realize clearly that Pan Americanism must not and cannot be thought of solely as a bulwark for isolation but as a road leading to more efficient universal co-operation.

"The peace of Europe," said a Cuban internationalist, Orestes Ferrara, only a short while ago, "is the peace of the Americas." The converse also holds true. No merely local settlement can be stable or final. Whether we like it or not, the modern world constitutes a single compact whole from which abstention is impossible. This being so, any formulas that we may adopt in this hemisphere, however valuable from the standpoint of defense, will yield their full fruits only when the other continents likewise organize on a basis of close interdependence, associating themselves in vast amphictyonies governed by the same law as that advocated by the Americas: the exaltation of liberty within a juridical system in which the sovereignty of the states shall at no time conflict with the general solidarity of the human race.

We have pointed out the need of co-ordinating the sovereignty of the different nations to establish enduring peace. If each sovereign nation delegates a minimum part of its sovereignty to a world court this means that, except for this voluntary contribution of a small fraction of its authority for the sake of mutual co-operation and to eliminate the possibility of war, its sovereignty will continue to be the foundation of its destinies, its liberty and its culture. These values, according to President Vargas of Brazil, constitute "a sacred sentiment intrinsic in the continental patrimony." To this sentiment, Sumner Welles referred in his eloquent address of February 16, 1942, to the Cuban Chamber of Commerce of New York:

"The bedrock upon which this new epoch of Inter-American understanding is founded is the recognition in fact, as well as in word, that every one of the twenty-one American republics is the sovereign equal of the others. That implies that interference by any one of them in the internal affairs of the others is inconceivable. Destroy or change that foundation and the inter-American federation which now exists will crash into ruins."

The defense of this sovereignty will, as in the past, be the guiding principle of each nation, but this defense will no longer depend on force alone, since already, as we can see in modern international relations, one of its firmest guarantees is its moral strength. Until the present war, for more than a century, small nations such as Switzerland, the Baltic countries, and Holland, commanded the respect of the world because of their exemplary national conduct.

For a nation to be respected it must be worthy of respect. Its best defense is the uprightness of its officials and its loyalty to its institutions and its pledged word. For this reason the essence, the supreme guarantee, of our inter-American life should be the maintenance of institutions of such moral nature as to win the respect of all nations. This guarantee will find its material strength and its spiritual consecration in Pan-American organization.

Despite the idealistic utterances of the leaders of the democratic nations as to the motives which inspire the democracies in their fight, we cannot lose sight of the fact that human nature always bears within itself the germs of aggression.

Unquestionably, thanks to the power of organization, the better human impulses will prevail over the forces of destruction. Our hope rests on this. Therefore we must strengthen the organizations that back up these principles of collective security. The union of America constitutes one of the most valuable contributions to the ideal of replacing brute force with the collaboration of nations, for it is not a new experience or an improvisation, but a well-advanced reality.

The philosophers of war will go on affirming with Treitschke, the teacher of Hitler and the Nazi youth, that it is a moral perversion to attempt to abolish war, which is mankind's field for heroic action; the same sort of thesis will persist as that which contends that the Aryan peoples have been, and always will be, able to defend with the sword what they have conquered by the spirit, and that the Living God will see to it that there are always wars as a "dread medicine" for the human race. This aggressive philosophy will go on contending that the universal state is an abomination, because the rays of divine light appear only in individual nations and that each presents a different image and concept of the divinity; on every favorable occasion, the strong will go on believing and affirming, in different ways, that war "is the only cure for sick nations."

Against the temptation of such ideas, the dream of peace has yet to make its way through the stodgy arrogance of the powerful. The close, enduring union of the nations of America will be one of the outposts in this struggle in the tireless defense of peace. The term pacifism is misleading. Defense of peace is a more adequate expression, for it implies the vision, ability and determination to fight: i. e., peace must be defended with both the holy word and the sword.

It would be well to note that it is not only the war-lords who are skeptical on the subject of the sovereignty of nations. "The bomber," wrote Stuart Chase, "together with other new inventions of destruction will greatly reduce the number of nations having full sovereignty. In 1939 these nations numbered 70. How many will there be left at the end of this war?" And he goes on to quote the words Lord Lothian wrote in November of 1939: "Although few are aware of it, the old anarchy represented by the multiple national sovereignties is on the point of disappearing. The great military powers, either by force or by the magnetic attraction of their own power, will bring together groups that were formerly self-governing with the promise of peace, security and prosperity in exchange for entering into their orbit. . . ."

Only a short time ago Sir Stafford Cripps, addressing the small nations, emphasized the importance of a federation of nations. To which Lord Cecil replied that the day of the sovereignty of nations was a thing of the past.

Therefore we cannot indulge in the optimistic belief that the concept of world peace and the equity of nations is an unanimously accepted doctrine. Those desiring such a state will have to remain girt for battle, and the defense of that doctrine will be one of the greatest privileges of united America. The powerful nations as well as the small must look upon it as their duty to fight for the noble ideal of a civilization resting on peace. To this end America has organized under the doctrine of Pan Americanism, a doctrine whose strength and guarantee reside in the fact that it is upheld by all the free peoples of America. Any defection or lack of enthusiasm involves not merely a national responsibility but a menace to the future of the continent.

Every day that the technique of destruction advances, war becomes mass suicide. The great powers need to be freed from armament races which exhaust their wealth and energies, and from the jealousies and provocations which lead to armed conflict. The small nations have everything to gain from a system which protects them against the aggression of the strong, and much to contribute. The support of the small nations strengthens the hand of international justice, because these countries are not moved by selfish or equivocal interests, but by the ideal of human solidarity, untainted by low opportunism.

Let us look back on the role Mexico played in the League of Nations. Mexico is not a great military power. At this moment it is a source of regret to me, because if she were, she could take a more important part in this struggle of the free peoples of the world against the despotisms. Nevertheless, at the table where the representatives of the nations of the world meet to discuss international problems, she has always thrown her weight on the side of right and justice against every attempt at international bad faith.

"What difference does Ethiopia's fate make to Mexico, with its limited scope of interests?" some asked as they observed the opposition of the Mexican delegates in Geneva to the plan to wipe a state off the map to satisfy a dictator's lust for empire. "Why does Mexico, not being a signer of the Versailles Treaty, oppose Germany's restoring obligatory military service and remilitarizing the Rhineland?" inquired others.

"Why does Mexico, since it voluntarily renounced the privileges accorded it in the China Treaty, so violently denounce the 'incident' of the South Manchuria railroad or the attack on Marco Polo Bridge?" asked still others.

"What are Austria and Czechoslovakia to Mexico?" This was the astonished question of those who did not understand or did not want to understand that these episodes were but the prelude to the catastrophe that was to engulf the world.

The thing that mattered to Mexico, even though she could lend only her moral support to the spirit of justice, was her alignment with the active forces upholding the great human ideals.

When in March, 1935, the government of the Reich decreed the rearming of Germany, in violation of the Versailles Treaty terms, Mexico, which had had no part in drawing up that treaty, raised her voice in protest, not only because of the unilateral rejection of treaty obligations which this step represented, but because she realized that the peace of the world would be seriously endangered.

About this same time, a meeting of the League of Nations was called to investigate the trumped-up charges of Italy against Ethiopia. Mexico's attitude won for her the epithet of "sanctionist." This was applied to her in certain circles under the mistaken belief that the position of the Mexican government was due to some animadversion against Italy or to a stubborn adherence to the letter of the law.

Nothing could have been more erroneous. It was love of peace, loyalty to the principle of the inviolability of a nation's political independence and territorial integrity, as well as fidelity to the obligations she had contracted that made Mexico unyielding in the defense of principles which unfortunately went by the board. With them went one of the League's noblest efforts: the attempt to establish lasting peace in the world.

In the two phases of the Sino-Japanese conflict, engineered by the Empire of the Rising Sun, the South Manchuria railroad incident of September, 1931, and that of the Marco Polo Bridge in 1937, the Mexican Government followed its unswerving line of conduct: condemnation of the aggressor and complete support of all the measures that were adopted or merely proposed to help China. Mexico has never recognized the puppet state of Manchukuo.

When Germany annexed Austria in 1938, in violation not only of various international agreements, but of a nation's right to decide its own fate, the government of Mexico was alone in its open protest of this act to the General Secretary of the League of Nations, of which Austria was a member. One of the duties of this body was to "maintain against all external aggression the territorial integrity and political independence of its members."

During the present war Mexico has protested the unjustified invasion by Germany of Norway, Denmark, Holland, Belgium, Luxembourg, Yugoslavia and the Soviet Union, as well as Italy's attack on France when the latter had been practically conquered by the troops of the Reich.

At the same time the Mexican Government, which steadily

adheres in its international dealings to the principle of not recognizing territorial conquests or de facto situations created by force, has maintained diplomatic relations with the governments in exile in London of the various invaded countries, Belgium, Holland, Norway and Poland.

Why? Because Mexico, moved by no selfish consideration, has constantly kept before her eyes the lofty principles toward which humanity has been striving in the hope of bringing about a harmonious, peaceful relationship among the nations of the world. Because she has wished to go on record as condemning the brutal aggression of the strong against the weak. And because, although at times she has been alone in this, she has sought to uphold the aspiration of the international community to live with equity and justice.

All this goes to show that the presence of countries such as Mexico, which are not great military powers, can be an indispensable moral force in the construction of a new world that will sincerely rest upon an enduring peace of collaboration and equality.*

N *Conclusion*

NEVER MORE ANGUISHED, THE HUMAN HEART searches the blacked out horizon for the future. Not only is the watcher depressed by the daily and tragic vicissitudes of war but by the awareness, sharpened by the present extraordinary means of communication, of the crags of uncertainty he will have to struggle through when peace arrives.

Unlike the greatest wars of the past, this total war brings physical martyrdom to all the peoples of the earth, not only by the bloody losses, but by subjecting them, under the destructive wave of radical changes in life, to violent upsets of economy, law and customs, and denying them all chance to grasp at any certainty.

We live under the lash of a hurricane that devastates all. What will tomorrow bring? Peace itself, when it comes—what

*Much of the material in this chapter appeared in an article by Dr. Padilla in the October, 1942, issue of *Foreign Affairs,* An American Quarterly Review.

will it mean for each nation and each individual?

These questions torture the imagination of statesmen, thinkers and the average man.

On the great canvas of the gigantic events this generation has experienced, two tragic realities loom like mountains: both war and peace.

The unsuspected magnitude of this conflict was not the quick-passing lightning stroke that some expected; instead each day that the war widens its reach, the anxiety over the final result grows proportionately.

The whole surface of the earth, feverishly exploited by both contenders, provides the sinews for resistance. The first duty is —win the war, for defeat would mean disaster, but the sacrifices to win the war take in, as never before in history, every aspect of human existence.

Every day, life suffers terrible dislocations. In this war, dictatorship, in the style of the Roman republic, converts itself into the centralization and the total regulation of life by the governments; and democracy feels itself shaken to its ideological foundations.

What animates the ranks of the democracies is the struggle for liberty, and each day more and more liberties vanish.

Nevertheless, necessity is a law; and war enforces unity of action, the resolve to win, and the discipline of souls. Discontent cannot be allowed to filter through the closed precincts of the fortress of collective sacrifice.

The war joins together all thoughts and all wills. But at the end of the war, these wills, like rivers discharging themselves into the sea, run the risk of being dispersed in anarchy. The greatest danger of all would be an improvised peace. Never will the nations be closer to discontent than the day after victory.

Behind this reality of total war, of this international conflict of extermination, in which two irreconcilable social philosophies are fighting to the death, the world has the feeling that it is living in a boiling social revolution.

What basically is occurring in the forge of contemporary history is a change in the methods of exploiting nature by which the conquests of technology enforce a substitution of power in behalf of human life so that these conquests do not serve to swell the profits of privilege, but become the patrimony of all mankind.

Irresistible new forces have been advancing: the growing power of organized labor, the rise of man to the first stages of political participation, and the already irresistible impetus to relate international life to the will and conscience of the peoples. Measures such as the dole and public relief are the expression of the might of the collective spirit which will not permit unjust sacrifice of the masses. An acquired right has mounted the platform of collective life: first of all, the right to labor, which soon is extended to the right of protection against adversity and the new right of every human being to live a decent life, even without work if unable to find it.

Technology has assured man dominion over Nature; mankind demands the right to share the advantages of this dominion. From every corner of the earth, in different tongues, in varying manners, louder than the voice of the leaders, comes the clamor for justice in unison on all sides.

The present war is swollen skin-tight with this contention. All that is debated is, in what form, in what mold, is to be emptied the hot liquid metal of this doctrine, of these public sentiments, all the resources within the reach of the peoples.

From what place is this movement, as driving as a flood, all this clamor for human redemption, to be directed?

Will it be directed from the fortresses of totalitarian despotism? Or will it be directed from the capitols of liberty?

The world already possesses a gigantic technique with which to produce the elements necessary for dignified human life; but there is one product, without which all others are rendered worthless so far as human happiness is concerned— freedom.

A certain day Buddha walked with his disciples through the steep mountains, when in the midst of the wild panorama, he saw a woman weeping bitterly. "Go," he told one of his followers, "and find out why the woman weeps."

"She weeps," replied the disciple, after making inquiry, "because some years ago in this same spot her father was devoured by lions, and because several months ago her husband was also torn apart by wild beasts, and because only a few hours ago one of her sons suffered the same fate."

"And why," asked Buddha, "does this woman insist on living in such a dangerous place?"

And the woman replied, "Because I prefer to live here rather than be subjected to the iniquity of tyrants."

This fable, old as history, contains a truth deeply rooted in the human soul.

The conflict which at present covers the face of the earth, has the same deep significance: the free peoples are challenging all dangers rather than submit themselves to the horror of a philosophy and a doctrine of government that represents iniquity and tyranny. But what men of good will should keep constantly in mind in these moments is that we should take advantage of these hours of suffering which infuse the human soul with eagerness and receptivity for universal justice, in order to construct the ideological bases of a fraternal humanity.

Modern war, which scatters disasters equally over all—trenches, open cities, soldiers, civilians, women, children—has unified the feelings of all men against the senselessness of armed struggles. And it has done something more, it has moved all hearts with a sentiment of justice and pity for the suffering of others. Nations which, like England, had lived for centuries immune to the sufferings of war on their own territory, now know what it means to have homes demolished and the lives of innocent and loved persons lost. Pain is the bridge over which human suffering may be approached in a Christian spirit. This, then, is the hour to create the ideas for the world of tomorrow. Once the devastating hurricane has passed away, on top of the widespread ruin will be reborn prosperity; and upon prosperity, selfishness, above all the selfishness of the strong. The voice of the great human multitudes who during the injustices of a badly organized peace suffer the same cruel uncertainties (made crueler still because of the lack of soothing hope) as the privileged peoples suffered during the war, will not be able to penetrate into the presidio of force which soon is converted into arrogance.

But for the present we all passionately hope for the end of

slaveries, the coming of fraternity, the abolition of poverty, and the enjoyment of liberty not only for the internal life of each country (which would be merely a new selfish imposture) but as the noble birthright of all men.

To provide—in answer to this clamor of the multitudes for justice, practical methods of production in abundance and just distribution, but always by methods guaranteeing freedom, is the pressing task not only of governments but of scholars, experts and leaders, of organizations, in short, of the peoples.

If the war demands unity of action, so does the organization of the peace.

If any of the constructive factors of the organization of peace gets out of hand, humanity will have to live an eternity of violence, of desperation, of bloody uprisings which will rush out like dark rivers of disunity and hate into a system of despotism.

Man, the final object of institutions, stands before the Sphinx, seeking the solution. And among the forces on which humanity counts for organizing the victory of the democracies in order to give it a human quality, free of hates, of prejudices, none is greater than America. Among the hopes upon which humanity counts to receive and direct the avalanche of peace problems, the most consistent, the most positive, is provided by the material resources, the methodic intelligence and the faith in the social doctrine represented by the solidarity of the American peoples.

Repeatedly I have heard it said: Can we have confidence in the present? But the future, who can assure the future? When men and circumstances change, what guarantees will the peoples of America have? What will restrain the United States, with all its economic and military power—especially as it will be organized after the victory of the democracies—from using its strength to dominate the rest of America?

I have attempted to show in these pages that the doctrine of Pan Americanism is not founded on altruistic motives, nor is it a policy that is upheld by the men or political parties that happen to be in power at the moment. This doctrine rests fundamentally on the reciprocal interests of the nations of America, on the practical realization that the objectives of imperialism and conquest, which were to assure markets and raw materials, can be achieved more profitably and safely through co-operation.

This doctrine is not the outcome of exclusively personal inspiration, but of the new international consciousness, which clearly and categorically condemns the policy of domination and exploitation of peoples. At the same time, its premises are based on the need of building up a new economy to replace the breakdown of the capitalist system under which we have lived. This economy must begin by restoring the purchasing power of the continent and by developing a material civilization which signifies not merely the acquisition of raw materials, but the creation of the spiritual unity of America as a bulwark against the insecurity of the future. Finally, the doctrine of Pan Americanism, which has had its trial by fire during the war, derives naturally from the democratic principle, which has passed beyond the frontiers of the individual countries of America to spread its concepts of equality and social justice throughout the continent.

A philosophy of fraternity, interdependence and humanity has become the standard under which the United Nations are fighting their war.

Therefore the interests of each country, the demands of modern science and of the new economy, the conscience of the masses of the people and the principles for which we have fought together, all combine to make of the federation of the peoples of America an indisputable reality.

The suspicion with which the United States is eyed in the carrying out of this Pan-American doctrine comes principally from old resentments sowed among the nations of this continent by economic systems, political groups, national and international philosophies which we, now united, are all combating in this world struggle.

But it is poor logic, short-sightedness and a lack of faith in man's destiny to persist in negative attitudes when the causes to which they owe their origin are disappearing.

With a criterion of this sort, nations, like individuals in society, would find themselves surrounded by enemies whom they would have to hate and fight, if the past brought them only thoughts of revenge, invasion and war.

This has been precisely the tragic destiny of the European nations. On this continent, each one of the nations bears the scars of the aggressions it has suffered at the hands of its neighbors.

Mexico has suffered at the hands of countries both of this continent and Europe. This is true of other countries and of nearly all those of America. But are we going to hug to our bosom this inheritance from the past which enslaves us and binds us to the yoke of a backward-looking, sterile hatred? In the Senate a short time ago I said, "A policy based exclusively on rancors from the past would be a paralyzed, blind, reactionary thing. The nobility of a civilization can be measured by its ability to forget injuries. Otherwise the world would never raise its head out of the dark jungle of evil passions."

The United States today stands upon a peak of history. It has been one of the founders of democracy in America and one of the creators of modern Constitutional law in the world. Under Lincoln it abolished forever the institution of slavery and proclaimed the dignity of the free spirit. Social justice and economic security have made amazing strides in the United States. The democratic philosophy which pervades its institutions and its education and the practices of its collective existence are proofs of a human understanding in which it is unsurpassed by any other country in the world. Nobody would say for a moment that the forces of evil are not strong in the United States. Perhaps stronger than anywhere else because they enjoy the benefits of organization which freedom gives. But this we can affirm: that the forces of good are stronger in this country than the forces of evil; that from this unending titanic struggle come forth the bountiful waters in which humanity can slake its thirst for human brotherhood and justice. The reason is, that in this nation one of the greatest populations of the world is gathered together and organized under the genuine inspiration of a true democracy, which has succeeded in establishing itself despite the abuses of its economic systems; and the people have been able, through the true exercise of their political rights, to maintain the right to pass judgment upon and change, if necessary, the path of the nation's destiny.

The great and formidable secret of the democracies is not that they never make mistakes—for democracy is probably one of the systems in which errors can most frequently occur—but that they can peaceably and with the vital conviction of truth learned through trial and error, take fresh bearings along the new paths that their people, fortified by education and the habit of freedom, have been following every day with surer and more invincible progress.

In the human struggle there have always been peoples who have been the guides up the rough slope of history. Just as Brazil is the guide in the spirit of fellowship, Mexico in social justice, the United States is the leader in liberty. Under these devices there should be no faint-heartedness.

The war we are undergoing has made one great contribution to the guarantees of equality and dignity in the carrying out of the doctrine of Pan Americanism. Its contribution is solidarity in the face of danger. A country like the United States that has traditions of honor, which lies under the noonday light of history, and whose people are clearly aware of the magnitude of the moment in which we are living, will never forget that, in these terrible hours of menace that beat down upon the world, but above all upon their own rich and powerful nation, all America, moved by a feeling of brotherhood, courageously put aside old futile resentments and, in the words of President Avila Camacho, gave one of the most telling proofs of solidarity that modern history can furnish: the joining of their destinies in the struggle against the totalitarian powers.

All these realities are what have strengthened the faith of the Latin American countries, a faith which is being translated into tangible facts and manly decisions; the faith that is needed on the march toward the future.

Above all else we should feel that we are Americans. The privilege of having been born on this continent lies in the fact that we have received no legacy of undying hatred; nor are we tormented by a thirst for revenge; nor are we tortured by differences of race. These exceptional circumstances make it possible for us to give shelter in a new civilization to humanity's hope of living in a world at peace, with freedom and social justice. The greatest mistake an American can make is to feel himself European, not American. This is not to participate in the building of a new world, but is to transplant to our shores the jungle of strife, disunity and fratricide from which his parents fled in search of brotherhood and union. This does not mean hating the land of one's origin; but the best way to love it is to bring into being in this new American homeland something our ancestors, oppressed by wars, tyranny, implacable hatred, never were able to enjoy, but which they would have wished for their children and all humanity: a civilization free from oppression, cruelty and poverty.

And we should consider it one of our paramount duties to raise on high the standard of Pan Americanism, knowing that it is the noble patrimony all our nations on this continent hold in common.

The Monroe Doctrine, despite the loftiness of its aims and the coincidence between its concepts and the declarations of the statesmen of the other American nations at that time, did not foster unity because of its onesidedness. We must see to it that the doctrine of Pan Americanism, which is the doctrine of the Americas, is not delivered over to the unilateral action of a single nation or a minority of nations of this continent. Whoever does not understand and carry out this reality betrays one of the greatest opportunities which history has reserved for each of the American nations and for the continent as a whole.

The Pan American doctrine is a fortress of dignity, of great mutual services, of democratic life, of enduring peace; of continental security, first, and finally, of world security.

Under the banner of this doctrine, defense and collective security will become an impregnable wall. It is then that America will be strong. In its natural resources it will find all the requirements for its needs, and in the souls of its people the noblest inspirations. Each man will have a purpose in living, a hope for which to fight, and a faith for which to die, if need be. Each of our countries will enjoy the supreme pleasure of shaping not only for itself and its own inhabitants, but for all the nations and for the coming generations, a noble, generous destiny. The remembrance of the sufferings the man of America has endured through so many slaveries, the contrast with a world in the grip of injustice, tyranny, fear of war, will strengthen his devotion and enthusiasm for a new American world which is co-operating in the peaceful organization of the whole world.

This will come not through the magic charm of a moment's effort; it will be an evolutionary movement which will demand steadfastness, enthusiasm and faith. But it will come. All the forces of the world in the war and after the war will join to give life to this impulse and make it fruitful. They will join forces to sow in the furrows, soaked with suffering and blood, the unification of the nations, and America must not be absent. The creative power of the new civilization is all-powerful. The gospel of co-operation, of man's redemption from the scourgings he has endured, the fight for the four freedoms Roosevelt speaks of, are alive on the American continent. We all have our part in this work; our faith is founded not only on the forces this new ideal has at its command, but in the powers of evil which we must combat.

Franklin said on one occasion that his country was where freedom was to be found, to which Morris responded: "My country is where freedom does not exist."

Both these thoughts underlie our resolve to build an authentic continental democracy which shall at the same time serve the nations which lack liberty as a blue-print for action and a stimulus in their progress toward the good life.

Thus the free man of America will have fulfilled his destiny.

Acknowledgement of Quotations

On the pages mentioned below, quotations from the following sources appear:

Page 10—THE LIFE OF LINCOLN, by Henry Clay Whitney, *Baker & Taylor, New York, 1908.*

Pages 41 and 42—MEIN KAMPF, by Adolf Hitler, *Houghton Mifflin Company, Boston, 1939.*

Page 48—THE OLD DEAL AND THE NEW, by Charles A. Beard and George H. E. Smith, *The Macmillan Company, New York, 1940.*

Page 95—LES TROIS GOUTTES DE SANG, by Elie Faure, *Malfere, Paris, 1929.*

Page 98—L'HOMME, C'EST INCONNU, by Alexis Carrel, *P. L. O. N., Paris, 1940.*

Page 102—CORTEZ AND THE CONQUEST OF MEXICO, by Bernal Diaz del Castillo, edited by B. G. Herzog, *William R. Scott, Inc., New York, 1942.*

Page 106—WINTER IN THE CARIBBEAN, by Paul Morand, *Flammarion, Paris, 1929.*

Page 107—THE INDIAN BASIS OF MEXICAN CIVILIZATION, by Dr. Manuel Gamio, *U. of Chicago Press, 1926.*

Page 157—SOVEREIGNTY AND FREEDOM, by Leon Duguit, from the Spanish translation by José G. Acuña, *Libreria Española y Extranjera, Madrid.*

Page 161—THE ROAD WE ARE TRAVELING, by Stuart Chase, *The Twentieth Century Fund, New York, 1942.*